Mass Murders

Bloodstained Crime Scenes Haunting the Bay State

SAM BALTRUSIS

Globe
Pequot

Guilford, Connecticut

Globe Pequot

An imprint of The Rowman & Littlefield Publishing Group, Inc.
4501 Forbes Blvd., Ste. 200
Lanham, MD 20706
www.rowman.com

Distributed by NATIONAL BOOK NETWORK

British Library Cataloguing-in-Publication Information available

Library of Congress Cataloging-in-Publication Data

Names: Baltrusis, Sam, author.
Title: Mass murders : bloodstained crime scenes haunting the bay state / Sam Baltrusis.
Description: Guilford, Connecticut : Globe Pequot, [2020] | Includes bibliographical references and index. | Summary: "Author Sam Baltrusis revisits the haunts associated with the most horrific homicides in Massachusetts, from the Lady of the Dunes mystery in Provincetown to the Lizzie Borden case in Fall River. Using a paranormal lens, Baltrusis delves into the ghastly tales of murder and madness to uncover the truth behind some of the Bay State's most bone-chilling crimes"— Provided by publisher.
Identifiers: LCCN 2019054663 (print) | LCCN 2019054664 (ebook) | ISBN 9781493049868 (paperback) | ISBN 9781493049875 (epub)
Subjects: LCSH: Haunted places—Massachusetts. | Murder—Massachusetts. | Supernatural.
Classification: LCC BF1472.U6 B3516 2020 (print) | LCC BF1472.U6 (ebook) | DDC 133.109744—dc23
LC record available at https://lccn.loc.gov/2019054663
LC ebook record available at https://lccn.loc.gov/2019054664

♾™ The paper used in this publication meets the minimum requirements of American National Standard for Information Sciences—Permanence of Paper for Printed Library Materials, ANSI/NISO Z39.48-1992.

Contents

CONTENTS

Foreword

Like so many of us residing in the twenty-first century, I've made many friends through social media. Among them is fellow paranormal author Sam Baltrusis. It was only a few years ago that we were cyber-introduced to one another by our mutual friend, Joni Mayhan, an amazing and prolific paranormal author, investigator, and sensitive. In 2018, Sam was kind enough to invite me to his Plymouth Paracon event in September, where I copresented with Joni.

It was my first paranormal convention, and to be honest I had no idea what to expect. While I had enjoyed successful sales of my books online, I had never been in the public eye, at least not as an author. Joni and I kicked off the event early in the morning. After a few minutes of audio difficulties and fumbling with a laptop to display our Powerpoint slides, we finally got our presentation started. When we raised our heads to begin, we found every chair to be full and several attendees standing in the open spaces in the back of the room. It was a packed house.

Joni had recently published *Haunted New Harmony* and I had just released *Haunted Tampa*. Joni came up with the idea for a dueling-style presentation where we shared stories from our books, trying to determine whose town was more haunted. It was fun and clever, as Sam's theme for the event was inspired by the show he appeared on called *Haunted Towns*.

While I didn't get to spend a lot of one-on-one time with Sam, I did see him quite frequently. Sam hosted a kickoff bash on the first night of the weekend-long event where para-celebrities gathered to meet their fans. The next day, I saw him frequently darting from one table to another fielding questions and seeing to his visiting vendors' needs. Wearing a dark suit, he wasn't unlike a shadow figure you might capture sight of out of the corner of your eye. In addition to scheduling the presenters, Sam had to plan the late-night ghost investigation. He had tirelessly worked to deliver a successful paranormal convention for all involved.

I had a blast presenting and answering questions about my experiences. Over the course of the event, I met a lot of online friends and sold every book I had brought with me. As the patrons asked me to autograph my books, I experienced a feeling of success I had, until that day, yet to enjoy.

For that experience, I thank Sam with all my heart.

During my interaction with friends and visitors interested in the paranormal, I fielded one question more than any other: "Did that really happen?"

Fueled by a mixture of cautious curiosity and startled disbelief, it's a question we've all asked in response to a story so fantastic that we challenge its validity.

As physical beings, we interpret the world through our senses. Our primary sense is sight. Seeing is believing. Our secondary sight is touch. Feeling something offers texture and temperature and elicits an emotional response, good or otherwise. In our modern and technological world, we rely heavily on our physical senses to provide us with proof and evidence of what is real. Unfortunately, this approach doesn't lend much to uncovering the mysteries of the nonphysical and paranormal world, especially when they're linked to violent murders and sadistic crimes.

Case files and witness statements often provide a sliding scale of truth regarding the details of an investigated crime scene. In some cases, continued investigations and new forensic technology can provide answers to lingering questions and even offer new evidence regarding the presumed circumstances of murder cases.

But what of the people, places, and things of the past that we can no longer see and touch? How do we reconcile the stories born from previous events, especially those involving gruesome and often unsolved murders? For those truly seeking truth, it's here that our physical senses must allow for the inclusion of a paranormal perspective, specifically in the form of psychic investigations and the occurrence of residual hauntings.

As I prepared to write *Ghost Crimes*, I compiled dozens of stories shared by both former and active police officers, emergency medical technicians, firefighters, and a retired detective. While the details of their stories were specific to their own personal experiences, they all contained an unexplainable paranormal element. For fear of ridicule, many of them tried to unlink their otherworldly experience from their minds and even official reports. As some got past the shock and awe associated with their brush with the paranormal, they allowed the memories of the unbelievable events back into their minds. Over time, they came to accept that while they may not have been able to understand why they had their experience, they believed that they owed it to the deceased as well as their family and friends to tell their story even after death.

If anyone is committed to honoring the memory of the dearly departed, it's my friend and author of *Mass Murders*, Sam Baltrusis.

If you have met Sam or are connected to him on social media, you are most likely aware of his deep love and adoration of the town of Salem, Massachusetts. Sam conducts tours of the infamous town, taking care to accurately portray not only the events of the early seventeenth century, but the memory of those so unjustly persecuted.

As a paranormal writer, I have a goal of entertaining my readers with a good ghost story. In the case of *Ghost Crimes*, the cases are based on actual events and weaved together in a fictional narrative. However, nonfiction stories carry an ethical responsibility to portray the deceased, their family, and everyone involved in a truthful, factual, and reverent light. To this end, Sam has performed countless hours of research and avoided telling of some of the more contemporary crimes out of respect for the victims' families.

Mass Murders dives deep into some of Massachusetts's most intriguing cases with painstaking care to identify and define the legends, history, and the residual hauntings associated with the crime scenes.

—Gare Allen, author of *Ghost Crimes* and *The Dead*

Introduction

Does a murder psychically imprint itself on a bloodstained crime scene? The mission of the book is to re-examine some of the Bay State's most horrific homicides using a paranormal lens.

It's a wintry, off-season night in Provincetown, Massachusetts, and I'm revisiting a string of mass murders that rocked the extreme tip of Cape Cod exactly fifty years ago.

Two cases in particular have haunted me for years.

Known as the spot where the Pilgrims first set foot on Cape Cod in 1620, it's no surprise that Provincetown, Massachusetts, is a hot spot for both tourists and hauntings.

Back in 2012, I spent the night at what turned out to be Provincetown's murder house. I was on assignment for a magazine and booked a weekend at the now-closed Victoria House on Standish Street. I was put into Room 4 and spent the night under my covers because I heard what sounded like muted cries or a whimper coming from a boarded-up closet. The following morning, I asked to be moved out of the paranormally active room. I intuitively knew something horrible happened there.

Years later I found out that the Victoria House had a dark secret. Back in the 1960s, the B&B was a guest house and was home to serial killer Antone Charles "Tony" Costa, also known as Tony "Chop Chop." He was convicted in 1970 of three of the seven murders of young women he's believed to have slaughtered, including Patricia H. Walsh and Mary Ann Wysocki. In the early 1970s, the house was often pointed out to tourists as the site where the killer lived. Costa then lured them to his "secret garden" of marijuana in Truro before murdering and mutilating them.

He met Walsh and Wysocki at the transient hotel on Standish Street. It's possible that he held them hostage at the guest house, which has been closed to overnight guests since 2014.

Costa's crimes were particularly gruesome. The hearts of each girl were rumored to have been removed from the bodies and were not found in the shallow graves. Of course, this grisly detail was probably exaggerated by the police. We do know that each body was cut into as many pieces as there are joints. Also, there were teeth marks found on the murder victims.

Kurt Vonnegut Jr. discussed the case in the July 25, 1969, edition of *Life* magazine, and the case became a national sensation.

"Jack the Ripper used to get compliments about the way he dissected the women he killed," wrote Vonnegut. "Now Cape Cod has a mutilator. The pieces of four young women were found in a shallow grave. Whoever did it was no artist with the knife. He chopped up the women with what the police guess was a brush hook or an ax. It couldn't have taken too long to do."

Vonnegut, whose daughter Edith had met Costa, talked about some "stained rope" found at the scene. The evidence was similar to the bloody coil found in Costa's closet in his Standish Street room. The author also captured the vibe of Provincetown in this well-crafted story, mentioning telling observations including graffiti painted on a Truro laundromat: "Tony Costa digs girls."

"In the guest house on Standish Street, near the center of town, the slain girls checked in for a night last January," the *Slaughterhouse-Five* author explained in the *Life* piece. "At the time, Tony Costa was renting a room there by the week. He was introduced to the other guests by the landlady, Mrs. Patricia Morton."

The female victims checked into Provincetown's murder house, but they never checked out.

Vonnegut corresponded with the carpenter turned murderer when he was incarcerated in Walpole. "The message of his letters to me was that a person as intent on being virtuous as he could not possibly have hurt a fly," Vonnegut said in his collection of essays and short stories called *Palm Sunday*. "He believed it."

As far as hauntings at the now closed Victoria House, there have been reports of a lingering, psychic imprint in Room 4. According to the hotel's former manager, he would hear disembodied whispers throughout the inn and the occasional scream of a female voice emanating from the serial killer's room. Some believe that Costa may have tortured his victims in the Victoria House similarly to Buffalo Bill in *Silence of the Lambs*, before murdering, mutilating the bodies, and then crudely dumping them in a shallow grave near Truro's Pine Grove Cemetery.

Serial killer Tony "Chop Chop" Costa met his victims at the structure currently called the Victoria House located at 5 Standish Street in Provincetown.

PHOTO BY SAM BALTRUSIS

The story almost became the crime of the century. However, Charlie Manson's "Helter Skelter" murder spree in California trumped Costa's chopping frenzy. The killer was sentenced to life in prison and ended up committing suicide by hanging himself in his cell on May 12, 1974.

During my visit to Provincetown in March 2019, I slowly walked by the Standish Street murder house and headed straight to Provincetown's cemetery. I was on a mission even though I was creeped out by the desolation of Commercial Street, the city's main drag. During the summer, the sidewalks are packed with revelers. In the winter, Provincetown is a ghost town . . . both literally and figuratively.

Based on my intuition, I strongly believe that there's a link with the "secret garden" murders in Truro and the Lady of the Dunes case, which happened six years later.

Any tie was ruled out because Costa committed suicide before the mysterious Lady of the Dunes was killed and found in 1974. In Costa's account of his role in the murders, he said that he had an accomplice named "Carl." Was this mystery man ever questioned?

When I talked with locals about the Costa and Lady of the Dunes murders, they said there were a few similarities, specifically in the mutilation of the bodies and the potential that they were sexually motivated. In fact, one year-rounder told me that she believes Costa's friend "Carl" played a role in the Lady of the Dunes death. While it's a far-fetched theory, I seriously believe we should reexamine these two cases using a paranormal lens.

It's been fifty years. Both cases need to be revisited.

PHOTO BY JASON BAKER

Located in the rear of the Pine Grove Cemetery in Truro, Massachusetts, is the brick crypt where serial killer Costa gruesomely dismembered the bodies of his victims.

The Lady of the Dunes, as she has been nicknamed, was found in a deserted service road hidden in the Race Point Dunes. On July 26, 1976, a teenage girl who was walking her dog discovered the naked decomposing body of a woman in her twenties or early thirties. The woman was lying face down with a pair of jeans placed under her head. A green towel was also found at the scene. She had long auburn or reddish hair in a ponytail, and she was approximately five-foot-six inches tall. She had an athletic build.

The female victim had extensive dental work done worth thousands of dollars. The killer had removed several of those teeth. Her hands had also been severed, and she was nearly decapitated and had received massive trauma to the side of her skull. Police believe she was also sexually assaulted. Her body has been exhumed twice, in 1980 and 2000, so forensic testing could be performed. No luck.

During my visit in March 2019, I found the Lady of the Dunes's grave marker. The headstone in Provincetown's Saint Peter's Cemetery is merely labeled "unidentified female." As I approached, I heard the sound of scampering feet and spotted a tiny figure dart by as I gasped for air. I was terrified.

At first, I thought it was a cat. And then, based on my past experiences with the paranormal, I assumed it was a cemetery-bound spirit. Or, as I joked to myself based on experiences with my book *Wicked Salem*, it could have been a ghost cat.

I lifted my flashlight and saw two eyes peering back at me. It was a red fox. We both looked at each other as I shivered in the beauty and the madness of the moment. If you believe in Native American shamanism, the fox is a spirit animal and an omen of sorts. According to native superstition, it's a warning of "dark magic" involved in an upcoming project. I quickly darted out of the cemetery and headed back to my room, located in Provincetown's West End.

It's no surprise I was put into the one room at the Province-town Inn that's allegedly haunted. I've stayed in this *Shining*-esque hotel with its killer views of the harbor many times since I moved back to Boston in 2007. I never scored the haunted Room 23 until recently.

It was after midnight, and, of course, I couldn't sleep a wink.

The wing I was staying in is usually off limits—unless the place is at max capacity or it's off-season. My room was facing the harbor, and I spent most of the evening transfixed by the view of the Pilgrim Monument and the water.

Unfortunately, I had no ghostly encounters at the Provincetown Inn that night. However, I did see what appeared to be an inexplicable shadow glide down the hallway one New Year's Eve night a few years ago.

When the team from the Provincetown ParaCon was on the hunt for a host hotel in May 2017, I immediately suggested the allegedly haunted Provincetown Inn. The three-day event was a huge success, and I assembled a motley crew of paranormal A-listers, including Provincetown's own Adam Berry from the Travel Channel's *Kindred Spirits* and Syfy's *Ghost Hunters*. At the paranormal convention, Berry accompanied Amy Bruni, his fellow investigator from *Ghost Hunters* and on-air partner from *Kindred Spirits*.

We held Saturday's main event in the hotel's Harborview Room. I had no idea it had a past life as a disco in the 1970s and a mafia hangout during the 1950s and 1960s. Eric Anderson, the group sales manager at the inn, told me he'd heard several reports of shadow figures darting past the storage area. "If we did have a haunted area in the hotel, it would be here," Anderson said, pointing to a room holding furniture and other anachronisms from the 1980s. "There was a disco in that room and all sorts of things happened here."

During our "true crime investigation" with Rachel Hoffman and psychic medium Lucky Belcamino, we did pick up some strange light and temperature anomalies in the former disco. After a spirited discussion with a longtime Provincetown resident who was friends with the town's notorious serial killer, Tony

"Chop Chop" Costa, we headed outside and had a close encounter with a possible hitchhiker ghost near the park commemorating the place where the Pilgrims first landed in Provincetown on November 11, 1620.

Jeffrey Doucette, cofounder of the former Haunted Ptown ghost tour, said the Outer Cape's most haunted locations have been turned into cozy bed-and-breakfast hideaways. "Provincetown is an old fishing community," he explained. "And when there's an old building with a weird historical backstory, there's potential for it to be haunted."

Over the years, Doucette has spent a lot of time crashing at the Provincetown Inn. Built in 1925, the West End haunt looks creepy, but Doucette isn't convinced it's haunted. "Every time I stay at the Ptown Inn, I expect the two girls from *The Shining* to show up," he joked. "But I haven't had a 'redrum' experience there yet."

However, he does think Provincetown boasts a higher-than-usual percentage of haunted guest houses. Why? Doucette, who was a veteran tour guide in Boston, said there's a distinct difference between the haunted hotels near the Boston Common, like the Omni Parker House, and the overnight dwellings scattered throughout Provincetown. "What's interesting about Provincetown is that a lot of the active old homes have been turned into guest houses. They weren't hotels or bed and breakfasts to begin with . . . they were homes," he said. "Provincetown's haunted corridor is Johnson Street with the Carpe Diem, Christopher's By the Bay, and a slew of others around the corner."

Doucette has a point.

My first face-to-face haunted encounter in Provincetown was at Revere Guest House on Court Street. Staying in Room 8 on the top level, I watched in awe as the door knob turned and I saw what looked like a nineteenth-century fisherman pass through the small hallway from neighboring Room 7. During a second visit, I heard what sounded like a single marble roll down the hall.

According to the inn's former owner, Gary Palochko, a sea captain named Jackson Rogers from the Azores owned the house in the 1860s and, during renovations in 2004, Palochko uncovered a nineteenth-century map.

When I mentioned my spirited encounter, the former B&B owner shrugged and said ghosts "scare customers away." However, he said that inexplicable noises heard by previous guests in Room 8 stopped once he found the map and other hidden treasures from the 1860s.

Based on historical research, there were three kids—Jennie, Manuel, and Joseph—in the Rogers family, as well as the fisherman's wife, Mary. Based on my experience and other reports, the paranormal activity sounded like a residual haunting, or a nonintelligent, videotaped replay of past events.

What about the weird sound I heard in the hall? The Revere Guest House's innkeeper sheepishly told me that he also uncovered an antique marble buried within the walls.

While Provincetown is a hotbed for paranormal activity, it wasn't always an open-and-shut case when it came to my search for the most haunted crime scenes in Massachusetts. Not every murder house is haunted. And not every victim turned psychic imprint is based on actual fact. In some cases, a horrific backstory

Located at the extreme tip of Cape Cod, Provincetown's year-round population averages a few thousand and swells by thousands during the summer. The dramatic increase during the warmer months doesn't include its ghostly inhabitants.

was completely fabricated or twisted over time to explain the supernatural.

With a few haunts featured in *Mass Murders*, I had to dig for the skeletal secrets buried deep beneath the Bay State's blood-stained soil. Based purely on its unsubstantiated lore, some locations didn't make the cut. However, it doesn't always mean there isn't some truth behind the legends.

Joni Mayhan, author of *Ghost Magnet*, believes that crime scenes have the potential for a residual haunting based purely on their bloody backstories. "I believe that locations of tragic events are more prone to a haunting than any other location," she told me. "When a person dies unexpectedly, sometimes their soul doesn't pass through the white light as it should. The emotions surrounding the event often make them balk. Sometimes when it happens suddenly, they don't even realize they've died. Other times, they remain because of a sense of guilt or a need to let others know what happened to them."

Mayhan researched the history of the S.K. Pierce Victorian Mansion in Gardner while writing *Bones in the Basement*. According to multiple psychics who visited the location, a female escort was killed in the house. "Supposedly, a prostitute was murdered in the red room of the haunted Victorian. Psychic mediums have picked up on her energy over and over again, giving the legend a sense of validity. However, no records show a woman who wasn't a member of the Pierce family dying in the mansion," Mayhan explained.

"Could it have been covered up? Certainly. Wealth and power would provide them with far more means than if it happened to someone of lesser fortune. Some people feel that it happened later in the mansion's timeline, during the time when it was a boardinghouse or perhaps when it was vacant. If this was the case, she wasn't a resident of the mansion, and her body was carried away before anyone could discover the murder," Mayhan continued.

Some crime scenes, she said, aren't haunted because the victims crossed over to the light. "I once invited my Paranormal 101 class to the murder site of seventeen-year-old Patricia Joyce. She disappeared in 1965 while taking a shortcut through the woods around Crystal Lake in Gardner," Mayhan said. "Her body was found thirty feet from the pumping station. It was the first murder in Gardner in fifty-one years and remains unsolved to this day."

Mayhan's class attempted to reach out to the spirit to help solve the cold case. No luck. "Several of my students are talented psychic mediums, and none of us were able to connect with Patty's soul. We believe she crossed over immediately, which is sometimes the case. Judging by the information we found in a blog that was written by her sister, Patty was a good girl who typically followed the rules in life. She probably wouldn't have resisted the white light and would have crossed over at the time of her death, like she was supposed to do. The imprint of her death was strong in the area, but we felt it was a residual energy that was absorbed by the location."

However, not every paranormal expert believes extreme violence psychically imprints itself into the environment.

Michael Baker, a scientific investigator with the group Para-Boston, said there isn't any rhyme or reason why a crime

The Lizzie Borden murder house, now a bed and breakfast, is located at 92 Second Street in Fall River, Massachusetts.

scene would be more paranormally active when compared to other Massachusetts-based haunts. "When we are speaking of interactions with activity alleged to be connected to the existing consciousness of human beings, I would think a more active history would always play a bigger role," Baker explained. "However, in my findings I have not yet seen a correlation between the type of historic activity and proposed hauntings. Much of the connections of violent pasts to haunted locations seems to be more folklore than fact. I'm still not sure what elements of our daily lives leave the biggest impact."

In other words, Baker believes that a place like Lizzie Borden's later-in-life home, Maplecroft, has as much potential to be paranormally active as the actual house on Second Street in Fall River, where the murders occurred. "The claims of hauntings by the majority seem to be void of elements that directly tie to major historical events," he said, using his data-focused NECAPS report as proof. "We never see Lincoln giving the Gettysburg Address for example, and while the battlefields in Gettysburg do seem to produce alleged remnants of battles, that trait does not seem to continue in many other violent locations where paranormal activity is simply footsteps or doors closing," Baker explained.

Are crime scenes more prone to paranormal activity? Yes, it's possible. After visiting many of the hauntings associated with the state's most heinous crimes starting with Cape Cod's Provincetown and then heading west to the Hoosac Tunnel in the Berkshires, I can say without hesitation that there's one absolute truth that recurs throughout the *Mass Murders* book: beautiful places aren't immune to brutal crimes.

CRIME PROFILE: ANDREA PERRON

> Bathsheba could never live down the accusations that
> were levied against her. Not only did she suffer in life,
> she suffered in the afterlife.
> —Andrea Perron, *House of Darkness House of Light*

Andrea Perron, author of the three-part *House of Darkness House of Light* book series, is on a mission. She's determined to clear the name of Bathsheba Sherman, a woman who was first demonized by her tight-knit community located on the cusp of the Massachusetts and Rhode Island border and was then vilified as a child-murdering demon spawn whose sewing-needle backstory was sensationalized by Hollywood in the first *Conjuring* movie.

According to Perron, the alleged murderess was a far cry from the blood-spewing villain that was portrayed on the silver screen. In fact, Perron believes that Sherman was targeted by

her nineteenth-century community and the witch hunt continues in the afterlife.

"I'm her great defender," Perron told me in an emotionally charged interview. "I have no way of exonerating Bathsheba of anything that she was accused of because I don't know for a fact if she did or did not have anything nefarious to do with what happened in that house. But she should be given the benefit of the doubt."

Hell hath no fury like a dead woman scorned? Think again.

"There's nothing recorded that substantiates the idea that she practiced witchcraft," Perron said. "If she did, it would have been a Salem-style death. As we saw with the innocent people who were hanged in 1692, *witch* was a dangerous word to say."

Bathsheba, whose maiden name was Thayer, was born in Rhode Island in 1812 and married Judson Sherman later in life in Thompson, Connecticut, on March 10, 1844. The most terrifying entity portrayed in *The Conjuring* movie was actually a real woman who had a son, Herbert, born in March 1849, when Sherman was thirty-seven years old. It's believed that she had three other children, and local lore suggested that they all died young. However, there's no proof to confirm the story.

It's been said that Sherman was a stunning beauty and lived next to the Arnold Estate in Harrisville, Rhode Island. When an infant mysteriously died in her care at the neighbor's farmhouse, the local gossip mill demonized her. It was determined during the examination that the child was fatally impaled by a large sewing needle and, even though Sherman was acquitted based on insufficient evidence, the court of public opinion somehow came to the over-the-top conclusion that the child was ritualistically sacrificed.

"Based on an article that my mother found, the men would look at Bathsheba with rapacious eyes," Perron said. "According to the community, she sacrificed the child in her care for eternal youth and beauty."

Was Sherman a devil-worshipping witch? Nope. Perron successfully shoots down the rumors in the third volume of *House of Darkness House of Light* in the "Season of the Witch" chapter. There's no way that she secretly practiced witchcraft, especially since Sherman was given a proper Christian burial next to her family. "She was buried in hallowed ground, and that wouldn't have been the case if she had been found guilty of witchcraft," Perron confirmed.

As far as her death, there are stories that Sherman "literally turned to stone" or was stricken with "a bizarre form of paralysis." Not true. Also, she didn't hang herself on a tree outside of the Arnold Estate, which was implied by the movie, after cursing all who would take her land. For the record, she died of old age on May 25, 1885.

For the *House of Darkness House of Light* author, Sherman's made-up backstory serves as a modern cautionary tale. "It's an example of how hearsay can become folklore and then ultimately become what some view as fact," she told me. "Words and rumors can cause harm. If something is repeated over and over, it can become fact."

Perron believes that Sherman's story was twisted over time because of the clothesline gossip passed down over the years. "There's no proof that she murdered anyone," she said. "I don't think we should accuse someone of murder unless we have empirical proof."

However, that didn't stop filmmakers of *The Conjuring* from creating a "based on a true story" account, which included a child-killing entity that attached to and then possessed Perron's mother, Carolyn.

"The movie version of Bathsheba was literally conjured by the minds of two well-meaning screenwriters," she joked. "That's what 'the conjuring' means to me. The story was embellished and pulled directly from Ed and Lorraine Warren's case files. The screenwriters tried their best to integrate true elements to the screenplay, but I had no control over it. I was a consultant on the film, and I was contracted as such, but it doesn't mean they listened to what I told them."

After being tipped off by local paranormal investigators Keith and Carl Johnson, the Warrens visited the farmhouse the night before Halloween in 1973. "The Warrens came about five times to the farmhouse to conduct an investigation over a period of one year," Perron said. "Mrs. Warren spent time with my mother, and Ed spent time interviewing us about our experiences and taking notes. We had no problem telling our stories to them. They felt safe to us. But they realistically only spent hours investigating our home."

The family's connection to Sherman's spirit came at the suggestion of the Warrens. Perron's mother told Lorraine about an incident that happened on the couch when they moved into the farmhouse in the early 1970s. Carolyn said that she felt a jabbing pain in her calf and then her muscles started to spasm. In *House of Darkness House of Light,* the author described the wound as a "perfectly concentric circle" and, based on the shape of the bloody puncture, it appeared as if "a sewing needle had impaled her skin."

Initially, the family didn't blame Sherman as the spectral attacker until the Warrens entered the Perron family's farmhouse on Round Top Road in October 1973.

"Mrs. Warren put her hand on the corner of the black stove in the kitchen and she covered her eyes," Perron told me. "She said, 'I sense a malignant spirit in the house and her name is Bathsheba.' I'm not saying that Bathsheba wasn't attached to the house, because I believe she was. However, there were many spirits in the farmhouse that presented themselves to our family over the years."

Perron said her childhood home was a "portal that was cleverly disguised as a farmhouse." In other words, a more sinister entity could have been responsible for the horrors that were lurking in the shadows of the Arnold Estate. "Lorraine kept saying it was Bathsheba," she said. "We think the spirit that was causing my mother grief was one of the original builders of the house."

The Perron family's association with the Warrens ended in 1974. However, the hauntings continued. "There were numerous things that happened there that the Warrens didn't experience," the author said. "There's some kind of male entity that is brutal. It's the same one that grabbed my sister Cindy by the hair. She went through hell in that house."

Because of its proximity to the Massachusetts border, which has a hush-hush history of land disputes, Perron believes there were undocumented deaths that happened on the property. "To give you an idea, my father paid taxes in Massachusetts because sixty acres crossed over the border. We do know that the land was fought over, but we don't know if there were casualties caused by the conflict buried on the property."

Perron said her younger sister Cindy was traumatized by the trapped souls of soldiers she believes were killed on the land. "Cindy would sleep in my room. The voices she would hear were overwhelming to her. There were seven soldiers that kept coming to her," she said. "The property has a very extensive history that we don't know about because it wasn't recorded. We don't know how many people died on that property, but we do know that at least a dozen spirits were in the house."

One horrific death involved the rape and murder of eleven-year-old Prudence S. Arnold. According to the official death record, her throat was cut by a farmhand after she was sexually assaulted on January 31, 1849. The homicide happened in neighboring Uxbridge, Massachusetts. However, because the property crossed the state border, it's possible that the murder could have happened on the Arnolds' land.

"We don't know much about Prudence's backstory," Perron said. "My mother worked laboriously and filled an entire notebook with all sorts of research. It detailed a lot of paranormal activity that included fairies and spirits as well as all of the deaths that happened on the land."

Unfortunately, the Warrens confiscated Carolyn's book of research. "My mother counts it among her greatest losses in life. Lorraine felt it was a haunted item that needed to be taken from the house," Perron told me. "When I confronted her forty years later, she said that she was protecting us. My mother turned it over to her in good faith, but I truly believe in my heart that Lorraine was a kind and loving person. It's best to let go and let God."

Sadly, Lorraine Warren passed on April 18, 2019. She was ninety-two.

There has been a renewed interest in the farmhouse that has serendipitously coincided with Warren's passing. Cory and Jennifer Heinzen, a couple from Maine, purchased the haunted property during the summer of 2019, and a slew of television shows, including the Travel Channel's *Ghost Adventures* and *Kindred Spirits*, reached out to Perron and asked her to recount her family's story on camera.

When I asked the author how it felt to return to the house from her childhood, I was shocked by the response. "It's been absolutely wonderful," she told me. "I don't know if you have ever been hugged by a house, but I have. I feel very welcomed in the farmhouse."

Perron said she has connected with the spirit that was negatively portrayed as a demonic entity in *The Conjuring* film. "When we did a spirit box session a few years ago, I heard Bathsheba again, and it was a voice that sounded familiar to me," she said. "What came through was a childlike voice. She was diminutive, almost like a pixie. We made sure that it really was her and then [the investigator] asked her, 'What one word do you associate with Andrea?' and I will never forget her response."

Perron started to get emotional when she recounted the spirit box session and her communication with the historically marginalized woman. "She said, 'Love,' and it was clear as day," she said tearfully. "It's because I told her story to the best of my ability."

Based on her experiences interacting with Sherman's spirit, Perron strongly believes that Bathsheba wasn't a bad person. "I think she was a sad and angry woman, and she had every reason to be," Perron emoted. "Bathsheba could never live down the accusations that were levied against her and the whispers that were said behind her back. Not only did she suffer in life, she suffered in the afterlife."

Mass Hysteria: Haunted Asylums

*The most haunted crime scene in Massachusetts? I was standing in
the middle of New England's deepest, darkest secret.*
—Sam Baltrusis, author of Mass Murders

I don't do asylums. But I finally got the nerve to walk through what's left of the Metropolitan State Hospital in Waltham, Massachusetts. The former psychiatric facility opened in 1930 and quickly earned a not-so-stellar reputation for its sadistic, over-crowded conditions. The hospital's Gaebler Children's Center, for example, reportedly medicated its patients to an extreme, which, based on local legend, resulted in multiple fatalities.

And then there was the heinous "hospital of the seven teeth" homicide. In 1978, Ann Marie Davee was murdered by copatient Melvin Wilson. He dismembered her body and buried pieces of the corpse in several shallow graves scattered on the grounds of Met State. Wilson also kept seven of Davee's teeth, which he tucked away as sociopathic souvenirs. Two years after the murder, on August 12, 1980, Wilson escorted police on a sick and twisted tour of the hospital's grounds, showing police where he buried pieces of Davee's dismembered body.

PHOTO BY JASON BAKER

The Metropolitan State Hospital was a large American public hospital for the mentally ill and is believed to be the inspiration for *American Horror Story: Asylum*.

It should be no surprise, but it's said that *American Horror Story: Asylum* was inspired in part by Met State's dark, mental patient past.

Laura Giuliano, an investigator with Para-Boston and a regular visitor to the Lexington portion of Met State, warned me about the haunted crime scene that has been converted into a luxury apartment complex. She believes there was evidence of a potential cover-up at the former asylum. "It sounds like it came straight out of a horror film . . . except it's true," Giuliano told me.

"Can you imagine a fifty-seven-year-old man who has been in mental facilities since he was seventeen having complete access to a thirty-six-year-old woman who has been in mental facilities half her life? Based on the facts of the case, he was freely traipsing around the woods on the grounds of the hospital property and had the time to make a hut, kill this poor woman, have access to a hatchet, cut her up into pieces, pull out seven of her teeth, bury her in three holes, and return to his room with seven of her teeth," Giuliano said.

"If that is not horrific enough, Met State hospital employees noticed Miss Davee was missing and didn't respond," she emoted. "The next day they decided to look for her. They found a hut, clothes, and bed linens in the woods, and within a day they disassembled the hut and washed the linens," Giuliano continued, adding that it was a "sad and sick story on so many levels."

When I first started writing historically based ghost books back in 2011, I swore I would stay far away from the horrors that unfolded in the series of former asylums scattered throughout Massachusetts. The two that terrified me the most were Met State and Danvers State Hospital. Ironically, both former psychiatric facilities have been renovated by the present-day owners, Avalon Bay. As an empath, the lingering energy was too much for me to handle.

I somehow picked up on the negative fingerprints left behind at the various locations I often visited during the research phase of my books. The trauma of the thousands who lived and died at these inhumane institutions has somehow psychically imprinted itself into the environment. If I went to the former asylums, I believed, I would relive the pain. In a worst-case scenario, one of the lost souls would follow me home.

Based on firsthand experience, some attachments with a tortuous history are nearly impossible to shake. A murderous entity hitching a ride with me? Not today, Satan.

In addition to my intense fear of Met State, I've been terrified to even get close to one asylum that has been featured in the

PHOTO BY JASON BAKER

Author Sam Baltrusis investigated many of the haunted locations featured in *Mass Murders*, including the Metropolitan State Hospital in Waltham, Massachusetts.

cult-horror flick *Session 9* and served as the inspiration for the infamous Arkham sanatorium from H. P. Lovecraft's "The Thing on the Doorstep." Yes, the complex has been closed for years and converted into upscale apartments. However, there's an inexplicably dark energy lurking in the shadows of the Kirkbride building edifice and the two cemeteries located behind the hospital's grounds.

The Danvers State Hospital, also known as the Danvers Lunatic Asylum, was built on the property owned by Salem Witch Trials magistrate John Hathorne and opened in 1878 after four years of construction. Using the supposedly more-humane "Kirkbride plan," which resembled the wings of a bat and housed numerous buildings that sprawled outward from the center, Danvers State Hospital was designed to hold under 500 patients, but its population reached over 2,000 by the 1930s.

Because of the severe overcrowding, patients were put into "special garments," presumably straitjackets, as a means of control. By

1948, the first lobotomy was performed at the psychiatric hospital, and electroshock treatments were introduced as a form of therapy.

It should be no surprise that the horrific conditions resulted in numerous fatalities. In fact, a report released in the late 1930s suggested that at least 400 patients died from unnatural causes. For example, two hospital attendants were sentenced to jail for the beating death of a man committed to the asylum. On September 28, 1934, several people became ill and one died after eating a sauce that was laced with insecticide.

The violence reached a fevered pitch in the 1950s, when two patients were beaten to death by a crazed mob in 1952 and then the hospital laundry superintendent, Lesley N. Jackman, was robbed and murdered by two young patients in 1955. The mysterious deaths continued until 1987, when one woman, Ann Houghton, wandered out of the hospital and was found dead the following day just 200 yards from the facility after suffering what appeared to be a heart attack. There were also reports of violent attacks and rapes, which ultimately resulted in the closing of the Kirkbride complex in 1989.

After an order to end state-operated hospitals, the psychiatric facility was officially closed on June 24, 1992, and the remaining patients were moved to the nearby state hospital in Tewksbury.

There were two mysterious fires that nearly destroyed the facility. In 1941, a large fire broke out in one of the barns on the hospital grounds. On April 7, 2007, another fire broke out on the property and burned down most of the newly constructed buildings, and the intense heat of the fire singed the remaining Kirkbride spires.

While the former asylum has been repurposed as an upscale residential community, the ghosts from Danvers State Hospital's past continue to linger at Hathorne Hill. Ellen MacNeil, cofounder of S.P.I.R.I.T.S. of New England and featured investigator on the Travel Channel's *Haunted Case Files*, told me that a former tenant she chatted with heard all sorts of stories from Avalon Bay's staff. "The custodian said that Danvers was crazy haunted," MacNeil said, recalling an incident involving a couple that just moved into the repurposed asylum building. "They were all excited and planning a party. All of a sudden, two champagne glasses lifted in the air and clinked together. They moved out the following weekend."

My friend Brad's mother stayed at the Danvers State Hospital from 1976 to 1982. He said that some "pretty horrific stuff happened there," but he thought the asylum's Gothic aesthetic was stunning during its heyday. "Some of the walls were up to two feet thick and very well built," he told me. "It took them almost a year to tear it down."

Brad said that he got physically ill the last time he visited what's left of the Danvers State Hospital. "When I was walking up to the building that's left standing, which is the old administration building, I felt hot and then light-headed," he recalled. "I got out of there real quick."

Brad told me that you can't go near the cemetery hidden down a path near the apartments. Of course, that's the first place I headed to when I recently visited the complex. I was investigating a case involving a gravestone taken legally from the cemetery in 2000.

Danny Perez, a local artist and haunted objects collector, said that a former crew member from an independent horror film took home one of the numbered grave markers from the Danvers State Hospital's cemetery. "While filming, the groundskeepers were

PHOTO BY JASON BAKER

The unclaimed corpses of inmates who died in the Danvers State Hospital were buried in a cemetery behind the Kirkbride building, and their graves were marked with numbered stones instead of names.

noticed changing out some of the original gravestones of patients who died there," Perez said. "The original grave markers were damaged and replaced with new ones. A crew member asked if they could take one as a memento."

Apparently, he did take one of the cemetery markers home, and the crew member didn't think much of it until seventeen years later. The man, who lives in Vancouver, started experiencing paranormal activity in his home and couldn't figure out what was stirring up the negative energy. "Alarms were going off at all times of the day and night, chairs being moved, bad smells, house plants died suddenly," Perez explained. "He would come home and the lights were on. He said there was the constant feeling of being watched, and his dog started acting strange and would stare at nothing. Overall, his luck was changing for the worse."

According to Perez, the film crew member from Canada reached out to a psychic medium, and she quickly identified the source of the problem, which was the grave marker that he legally obtained while working on the made-in-Massachusetts movie. "This object had been locked up in storage for years and forgotten," Perez said. "Recently, it was rediscovered, taken out of storage, and displayed because of its unique history. I'm told that's when it all started to change."

When the medium visited the cursed man's home in Vancouver, she immediately headed to his office and claimed that there was a negative energy attached to the grave marker.

"He was going to simply discard or dump the item when the medium said 'no' because it could just as easily become someone else's problem," Perez continued. "It needed to be contained."

Perez obtained the object after filling out the appropriate paperwork, and it was eventually cleared by customs.

As for the Danvers State Hospital cemetery, I noticed that several of the grave markers were knocked over. While there has been a renewed effort to assign names to the numbers, it's clear that there wasn't much respect for those buried there.

For centuries, an institution like Danvers State Hospital was a literal dumping ground for New England's "undesirables" and those traditionally marginalized by the status quo.

Asylums, or institutions built for the poor, orphaned, sick, and mentally ill, were unfortunately a dirty secret from New England's dark past. "Locals have grown up believing that many of these sites are haunted. They are: if not by ghosts then by the twisted and shameful legacy of what happened in these places," reported Scott Kearnan for the now-defunct *Boston Phoenix* in September 2012.

Based on the intense residual energy at many of the former asylums in Massachusetts, it would make sense that many of the people who lived in these buildings left behind a psychic imprint of sorts, especially if neglect or trauma was involved.

One hypothesis, developed in the 1970s and known as the Stone Tape theory, speculates that an environment can absorb energy from a high-tension event, such as an untimely death or a suicide. The theory is a possible explanation for the alleged paranormal activity at the former asylums, which include lights flickering and inexplicable screams. A residual haunting is like a videotaped event that plays over and over. Residual spirits are not intelligent entities and can't interact with the living. However, it's possible that a few lost souls with the postmortem ability to interact still linger in these hospitals where they were formerly sequestered.

Rachel Hoffman, an investigator with the all-female team called Paranormal Xpeditions, said it's possible that an aura of disaster has psychically imprinted itself into the land and buildings, especially those that formerly housed tuberculosis clinics, poorhouses, or mental institutions. "We believe that asylums are higher in paranormal activity due to the amount of personal anguish suffered by the ill and also the nurses who were understaffed," explained Hoffman. "We oftentimes hear them going about their daily activities as if they don't know they're dead."

Hoffman appeared on Zak Bagans's *Paranormal Challenge*, during which her team investigated the extremely haunted Rolling Hills Asylum in East Bethany, New York. On the Travel Channel show, Paranormal Xpeditions captured a "class A" electronic voice phenomenon, or EVP, of a female voice saying, "Don't you ever do that," followed by what sounded like a straitjacket slapping down after a bloodcurdling shriek.

"We believe it was a confrontation between a nurse and a patient," said Hoffman. "I believe it was residual activity and probably repeats itself consistently because the patient is unaware that she has died."

The veteran paranormal investigator told me that the ghosts haunting old asylums are both intelligent and residual. "We have come across spirits that are nasty in nature and tend to carry on being aggressive even after death," Hoffman said. "We also run into child spirits, which are the ones to us that tend to be intelligent and receptive. We generally bring candy or toys as trigger objects to evoke a response. Kids love candy and shiny toys and usually approach us easily, as we have a mothering nature to our crew of all females."

When I visited Met State, I couldn't help but feel for the woman who was savagely murdered in the woods surrounding the hospital in 1974. Davee, who was admitted into Met State on December 1973, was granted a grounds pass by her treatment team the following August. She was missing for months until staff found a woman's skirt, pieces of cloth, a pocketbook, and a small zippered case tied together in a bundle. Inside the purse were sunglasses, a hatchet, and a collection of photographs with notes written to Davee.

Based on the evidence found at Met State by Giuliano and her team, I strongly believe there's a lingering psychic residue at the location. "We investigated inside one of the renovated Met State buildings in April 2013. We set up in the lobby of the building, and there was a gymnasium on the floor above us that we did not have access to," she said. "About an hour after beginning the investigation, our lead investigator was listening with headphones and something captured his attention. He didn't want to say what it was, but instead passed the headset around for us all to hear. Everyone agreed it was clearly the sound of children singing. It was creepy singing, though. Not like an upbeat song, but a slow, eerie song like "Ring Around the Rosie." We couldn't make out their words, but it was extremely unsettling," Giuliano told me.

According to reports from the early 1960s, more than two dozen children died and were buried on the grounds. It's said that they were poisoned by strontium that doctors were adding to their milk, believing that it was a way to treat their mental illness. According to Giuliano and Para-Boston's case reports, the ghosts of these children are believed to still haunt the property. "Interestingly, it was after the investigation that we learned of the urban legend that sometime in the 1960s, two dozen children allegedly died from poisoning," she explained. "Because we were in a basement lobby at night with an auditorium and gymnasium above us with open access to all members, we could not unequivocally say we were hearing the spirits."

Ghost children singing "Ring Around the Rosie" at the former asylum? I'm convinced. Believe it or not, Giuliano has uncovered even more creepy evidence from this haunted location. "Months prior to our investigation, I wandered around the 330 acres of Met State," Giuliano recalled. "In a dense area, on the slope of a hill, I found the foundation of a small shack. Under many decades of composting leaves and brush, something white caught my eye. It was a

In 1978, Metropolitan State patient Anne Marie Davee was murdered by another patient, Melvin W. Wilson.

sheet. I uncovered it, and it said 'Property of Metropolitan State Hospital.' I couldn't believe it. A foot or two away, I found an old, outdated pair of brown women's leather shoes. The area was covered in poison ivy, so I took pictures and carefully ripped off the part of the sheet that contained the words of the hospital and took it home with me."

Giuliano said it was important to her to respect the victims from Met State's dark past. "I have covered over the area, and I've never taken anyone to it because if this was the area that Davee was murdered, I don't want her to endure any further desecration or disrespect," she said.

Based on the paranormal investigator's firsthand encounters, does she believe it's haunted? "If I hadn't heard the creepy singing of children with my own ears, I would not be so confident. Our investigation took place years after the condos were built, and we heard the singing," she said. "The employees that use the basement level have told me their paranormal stories, and I've heard stories from folks living in the new condos."

Giuliano continued: "Something is going on there. I hope it is just inexplicable energy caught in time and not spirits unable to move on."

As we talked, I fought to hold back the tears. I was shivering in the beauty and the madness of the moment. I had the ultimate realization. The most haunted crime scene in Massachusetts? I was standing in the middle of New England's deepest, darkest secret. It's Met State.

The Notorious

Maggie, come quick! Father's dead. Somebody came in and killed him.
—Lizzie Borden's words to Bridget Sullivan

Lizzie Borden and her sister, Emma, purchased Maplecroft in September 1893, after Lizzie was acquitted of murdering her father and stepmother.

Borden Murders

When it comes to untangling the myths and misconceptions surrounding the savage butchery of Andrew and Abby Borden that fateful August morning in 1892, the devil is in the details.

Pat Spain, host of the Travel Channel's *Legend Hunter*, revisited the case that rocked Fall River in a comprehensive exploration of the infamous whodunit in a television episode called "Lizzie Borden, Innocent?" which premiered in January 2019.

"It's widely accepted that Lizzie Borden, Andrew's youngest daughter, was the killer," Spain reported from the Superior Court for the County of Bristol in New Bedford, Massachusetts. "She was tried at the time in this courtroom and found not guilty. Now, there's brand-new evidence, new studies, that say Lizzie did not do it. If she didn't do it, then who did?"

Borden was brought in for an initial inquest hearing on August 8, 1892, which was four days after her father and stepmother were brutally slaughtered. Adding fuel to the fire, her trial started June 5, 1893, and another hatchet homicide happened in Fall River around the same time. The victim was Bertha Manchester, who was found murdered in her kitchen on June 1, 1893.

The Borden trial lasted about two weeks, and a verdict was reached after a quick deliberation. She was acquitted by a jury of her peers; however, the court of public opinion wasn't convinced.

"Lizzie's acquittal became a shock to the public," Spain explained. "After her release, she was demonized and taunted by everyone in Fall River. In the century that has passed since, almost everyone has Lizzie as a woman who got away with murder."

Did Borden actually kill her parents? Dr. Stefani Koorey, publisher and editor at Peartree Press, isn't convinced. "It was impossible for her to be the murderer," Koorey told Spain. "There was no time for her to clean up. She would have been drenched in blood. Lizzie lived her life without a sense of guilt. Her probability of guilt was under twenty percent."

Despite the acquittal, Borden never shook her "forty whacks" claim to fame. For the record, Borden's stepmother was struck nineteen times with a hatchet, and her father suffered eleven blows on the couch. Yes, the schoolyard rhyme was off by ten whacks.

Based on the extreme overkill, one expert featured on the program believes that Borden's older sister, Emma, had the most convincing motive. Both sisters were worried about losing their inheritance, but it was Emma who approached their father about the issue. "Andrew Borden's Swansea estate was at the center of a family feud," Spain explained on *Legend Hunter*. "It was rumored that Andrew was giving the Swansea farm to his wife, Abby—Lizzie and Emma's stepmother."

When Spain questioned scholar Shelley Dziedzic about Lizzie's older sister, she believes Emma had the rage needed to commit the horrific crime even though she had a solid alibi. "She was nine years older than Lizzie and had strong memories of her mother, Sarah," Dziedzic said. "It was Emma, not Lizzie, that went to the father."

Emma was at the Brownell House in nearby Fairhaven on the day of the murders. However, the older sister's personality based on Dziedzic's interview seemed to fit the profile of someone capable of committing such a heinous attack.

Thomas Hodgson, the sheriff of Bristol County, told Spain that the Borden murders were unusually cruel. "The killer had to have had such rage and anger, but then to wait an hour and then to go and commit the second murder would suggest that there's some sociopathic issues involved," Hodgson said. "People who have those tendencies tend not to even see themselves as having committed that first murder. They immediately separate themselves into a different reality."

Bill Pavao, a Borden historian who was curator at both the Second Street house and Maplecroft, weighed in on John Morse and his association with the murder. Pavao cleared up one myth that has been perpetuated by unsubstantiated rumors, specifically that Morse was implausibly specific about his whereabouts on the day of the murders. "There's really no documentation," Pavao told Spain. "I think it's been embellished over time."

One fact that has been lost is that Morse slept on the third floor, which is a present-day bathroom, when he lived at the Second Street home. On August 3, 1892, he slept in the now-infamous second-floor guestroom where Abby was killed. "Maybe he was staying there to give Abby a reason to come up there the next day?

It's interesting that the night of the murders he went back up and slept in that room in that bed," Pavao told Spain.

Yes, it's extremely strange that Morse slept in the crime-scene room where Abby was hit eighteen times to her head and once between the shoulder blades.

It was after Pavao's interview that Spain came up with the supposed bombshell that the murderer had to be left-handed based on the blows to the stepmother's head. The show suggested that all three of the suspects were right-handed, but Pavao told me after the premiere of the television program that he found a few inaccuracies in Spain's research.

"I feel like people need to keep the case simple," Pavao told me months after the premiere of the "Lizzie Borden, Innocent?" airing. "The left-handed theory assumes Abby was facing the killer. Also, Lizzie did have time to clean herself after Abby and would not have necessarily been bloodied by Andrew's killing. Lizzie could have reached around from inside the dining room doorway when killing Andrew. This would have allowed the wall to shield most of her body from the blood spatter except perhaps her arm."

Pavao said that there were several major inaccuracies highlighted on the show. "There's no evidence that the Swansea farm was the center of a family feud," he said, finding some huge holes presented as groundbreaking research. "Lizzie was not on morphine when she was first questioned. We also don't know the strength of the morphine she was eventually given."

Some of Spain's "tests" during his televised investigation were flawed. For example, there was a train that connected Fairhaven and Fall River at the time, so horse and buggy wasn't the only mode of transportation for Emma, which Spain painstakingly re-created.

Also, the show seriously wanted to prove Borden's innocence. "The question was not whether Bridget Sullivan could hear Andrew's murder, but could Lizzie hear Abby's body hit the floor? They didn't check this," Pavao said, adding that he did test this possibility when he lived in the Second Street home. "A 200-pound person hitting the floor would've been heard downstairs," he told me. "Of course, it depends on how she fell."

At the end of the "Lizzie Borden, Innocent?" television show, Spain summed up his investigation at the spot where all the Bordens who were involved in the murders are buried, Oak Grove Cemetery. "What I found is that I just don't want to believe that it was her. Despite what the experts have said, I just find it really difficult to accept that somebody that is capable of this kind of brutality, this heinous crime, could have close friends that genuinely loved them and start the humane society of Fall River," Spain concluded. "I guess it comes down to what you think of Lizzie Borden as a person."

Pavao, who pointed out that Borden didn't start Fall River's humane society but did fund a local animal rescue group, believes that the team from *Legend Hunter* didn't intentionally revisit the Borden case with a biased lens. "Pat Spain and the crew were nice and professional. I like that the show focused on the history," Pavao said. "The problem is that people don't want to believe that Lizzie could have done it, so they spin the case."

While Pavao did find some inaccuracies with the "Lizzie Borden, Innocent?" television program, he said Spain did an overall excellent job exploring the complexities of the case. "I'm not being critical. I was glad to see and be a part of the show," Pavao said. "In the future, my wish would be that people focus more on the case itself, the characters, the history, and of course, the mystery."

BORDEN'S HAUNT: LIZZIE BORDEN B&B

FALL RIVER, MA—I didn't want to do it. The idea of spending the night at a location that I believed was one of the most haunted in New England was enough to send shivers down my spine. In fact, I chickened out of two previously planned overnight stays at the Lizzie Borden B&B before finally burying the hatchet during a visit in July 2017.

Then I started having the dreams . . . again. I've had them in the past, but the latest involved an unlikely player in the horrific double murder that rocked Fall River. The Bordens' maid, Bridget Sullivan, was reaching out to me when I was asleep. Her specter was pinning me to the bed, showing me what had unfolded that infamous August morning.

According to Sullivan's court testimony, she was taking a nap in her third-floor room after allegedly cleaning windows when Lizzie's stepmother, Abby, was savagely murdered in the second-floor guest room. Sullivan, nicknamed "Maggie" by the Borden girls, ascended a separate stairwell, avoiding the crime scene in the present-day John Morse room.

At 11:10 a.m. on August 4, 1892, Bridget heard Lizzie call from downstairs, "Maggie, come quick! Father's dead. Somebody came in and killed him."

In my dream, Sullivan kept pointing to the closet in her bedroom. She was trying to show me that there was a well or cistern in there, and, for some mysterious reason, the closet was significant.

My overnight stay at the Lizzie Borden B&B was quite an emotional tour de force. Within the first few minutes of walking into the house, I saw a shadow figure dart past the murder couch and heard a female voice say my name. For the record, the spirit had a very thick New England accent. My friend Lucky Belcamino, the official psychic of the haunted hot spot who recently relocated to Mississippi, was giving readings at the inn during my mid-July visit, and she filled me in on the hauntings.

Based on more than a decade of personal experience, the psychic medium told me that the activity in the house is amplified in the weeks leading up to the anniversary of the double murders.

"I do believe that during the summer months, when there are a lot of people booking rooms and attending the tours, the spirits are curious and love the energy in the home," Belcamino said. "They will be more apt to communicate with those that are respectful and want to know the truth."

Within the first hour, I visited the John Morse crime-scene room, and I was literally brought to tears by the spirit of Abby Borden. Based on her portrayal in pop culture, I always thought she was a wicked-stepmother archetype. I was wrong. Her energy was sweet, and the sadness I felt was somehow related to how Lizzie and her sister, Emma, hadn't accepted her as a mother figure.

Based on my overnight stay, I can safely say that the Lizzie Borden B&B has somehow become extremely haunted. But was it related to the murders or to something else?

Ron Kolek, author of *Ghost Chronicles* and longtime paranormal investigator, told me a theory a few years ago as to why certain locations seem to become progressively more paranormally active once they appear on TV. Are investigators—like the team from the Travel Channel's *Ghost Adventures*—somehow stirring up activity in locations that hadn't previously had histories of paranormal shenanigans?

"Look at the Houghton Mansion," Kolek told me. "I investigated that place years ago, before it became a regular location for paranormal groups. I've gone back there recently, and it's completely different now. There's stuff there now that wasn't there before. I think these paranormal teams are bringing something with them," he said, alluding to para-celeb investigators who somehow conjure negative energy at Houghton Mansion that didn't exist years ago. "Are they bringing stowaway entities with them? I think so," Kolek continued. "It's like negative spirits know where to go to get more attention."

My first thought after chatting with Kolek was about the Lizzie Borden B&B. It's one of those locations with reported paranormal activity that has become progressively more active, even sinister, over the years.

Although she was tried and acquitted of the gruesome murder at her 1845-era Victorian home on Second Street in Fall River, the hatchet-wielding Lizzie Borden never shook her "forty whacks" claim to fame that she hacked up her father and stepmother on August 4, 1892. In addition to her chop-chop notoriety, Borden has been rumored to have had an intimate relationship with actress Nance O'Neil. However, this scandalous affair is unsubstantiated.

"We don't have any real evidence regarding Lizzie's orientation," said Bill Pavao, historian and former curator at the Second Street house. Pavao actually lived in the home for several years before it became a recurring location on all the television investigation shows. He told me that he'd never experienced anything paranormal during his long-term stay.

However, my psychic-medium friend Lucky Belcamino said the vibe in the home has changed in recent years.

"I connect on a more personal level with Lizzie and the uncle, John Morse," Belcamino said. "I will sit in their rooms and do spirit-box sessions and talk to them like I'm talking to friends."

When the psychic medium asked Lizzie what she was doing during the double homicide, Borden's spirit told Belcamino that "she was eating six pears," Lucky said. "She's playful at times and sometimes a little rude and abrasive. Sometimes she will not say anything."

As far as ghosts are concerned, visitors claim to have heard sounds of a woman weeping and have spotted a full-bodied apparition wearing Victorian-era clothing dusting the furniture. Phantom footsteps storming down the stairs and doors mysteriously opening and closing have also been reported. Also, guests have heard muffled conversations coming from vacant rooms. Perhaps it's the spirits of Borden and Sullivan making a postmortem pact to hide the bloody hatchet.

Or, maybe it's something more sinister?

In my opinion, the basement is the most active location in the house. In fact, when I first opened the door after midnight, I heard a loud hissing, and my group of amateur investigators captured an

EVP of what sounded like nefarious laughter. When we played the clip over and over, the file mysteriously deleted itself.

Earlier, a guest I met from New Jersey captured video of what looked like "paranormal darts," or light anomalies, that moved around the area downstairs where the Borden's privy was located. There have been multiple reports of a sulphur smell in the basement, and it's believed that the house's cellar dweller could be an evil entity. Adding to my fear of spending the night at Fall River's murder house, the group from New Jersey fled the house at 5:00 a.m. after coming face-to-face with something that terrified them during our investigation.

In addition to my more recent dream involving Bridget Sullivan, I've had spirit communication dreams about the location that began long before I finally visited the haunted crime scene.

In one dream, I saw a man wearing 1800s-era clothing and facial hair walking into a house with flowery wallpaper. He removed his hat and sat on an old-school couch. The dream looked like a black-and-white 35mm and unfolded slower than the typical silent-era film. Before the man could rest his head, he looked at me, and subtitles appeared, as if I were watching a movie scene from the early 1900s. A woman emerged from the dining room holding a hatchet behind her back.

The subtitle that appeared in the dream has haunted me for years. It read: "Diablo did it." Then I woke up.

I didn't figure out the correlation between the house and my dream until my first visit to the Lizzie Borden B&B while on assignment for a magazine, which preceded my initial overnight stay by six years. At that time, I was more interested in trying to solve the murder and was less focused on the cryptic messages sent from my subconscious.

In hindsight, my dream seemed to be implying that the murderer—whether Lizzie, Bridget Sullivan, or the uncle, John Morse—was possessed by an extremely negative entity.

When the crew from *Ghost Adventures* investigated the house in 2011, the most interesting part of the television show was the paranormal research by Jeff Belanger.

"Andrew and Abby weren't even the first two Bordens to die on that property," Belanger explained. "In 1848, Andrew's uncle lived in the house right next door. His wife went nuts and drowned her three children in a well. One lived. Then she took her own life with a straight razor—slit her throat."

The investigation explored the possibility of an evil entity and suggested that the "property is plagued with dark spirits." Based on my personal experiences in the house, I believe this theory is likely. The electronic voice phenomenon the team allegedly captured upstairs was terrifying to me. It said: "Keep on killing. Keep 'em coming."

Another message from the spirit box said: "Tell 'em about the girl."

Was the spirit-box communication referring to the heinous crime that happened next door?

The murder in 1848 has fueled debate about whether madness ran in the Borden family. The infanticide by Eliza Darling Borden was even brought up in Lizzie's highly publicized trial. It's believed that Eliza drowned her children in the cellar's cistern and then, possibly suffering from postpartum depression, took her own life by cutting her throat with a straight razor.

Just to clarify the family lineage, Lizzie wasn't a blood relative of Eliza and was connected to her only by marriage through her great-uncle Lawdwick.

The children, who died forty-four years before Abby and Andrew were murdered, are rumored to haunt the land next door to the Lizzie Borden B&B. Guests leave dolls and other toys for ghost children who are believed to inhabit the guest rooms. Children have been heard laughing when no children are present.

During my first overnight stay in the Bridget Sullivan room on the third floor, I felt a disembodied hand touch my back. Others have reported that the chair in the room has moved while they were asleep, and the tour guide, Richard Bertoldo, said he has been pushed by an unseen force.

A possible explanation for the "tell 'em about the girl" spirit-box message captured during the *Ghost Adventures* investigation is that it could be a reference to the murdered child, Eliza Ann Borden, who was two when she was drowned in the basement of 96 Second Street.

In other words, "the girl" the spirit-box message was referring to may be a ghost child. I'm convinced the intelligent spirit on the third floor is a little one.

Lee-Ann Wilber, manager of the Lizzie Borden B&B, told the Biography Channel that it's common for guests to run out of the inn in fright. "I'm not used to picking up on things. They just sort of blend in now," Wilber said. "Nothing to drive me out of here."

However, in 2004 she was scared out of the house. She fell asleep on the parlor room's couch and woke at 3:00 a.m. and saw a shadow person. The old-school chandelier was responsible for the black mist in the hallway, she believed, but she also noticed a misty figure moving up the staircase.

"And as I'm looking at it, it walked up the staircase," Wilber told the Biography Channel. "I said to no one in particular, 'You win tonight,' and went to sleep in my car."

Wilber said she was a skeptic when she moved in more than a decade ago. "Living here," said Wilber, "very quickly, I became a believer."

Because of its gory history, it's no surprise that the Lizzie Borden B&B is believed to be haunted. Cold spots have been reported numerous times in the master bedroom where Abby came face-to-face with her cold-blooded killer. There's also lore involving a former maid who quit after seeing a body-shaped indentation on the bed in Abby's room.

My fear is that the *Ghost Adventures* lockdown may have stirred up negative energy within the house . . . or possibly brought in evil from outside the building. According to several sources, the place became unusually active after the investigation.

Rachel Hoffman from Paranormal Xpeditions agreed that the crew from *Ghost Adventures* potentially conjured activity. The paranormal investigator visited the property the day after the *GAC* lockdown. "I went to Lizzie's house and opened the door, and one hundred black flies flew out—grown flies," Hoffman explained. "They left six hours before."

Flies—and shadow figures—are common in a home that shelters an evil entity. Nausea, reported by Zak Bagans and Nick Groff on *Ghost Adventures*, is also a reaction to the presence of a dark force. Abby, Andrew, Bridget, and even Lizzie reported nausea hours before the two murders in 1892. Temperature fluctuations, specifically in a localized area such as the John Morse room, have been reported in other cases of infestation.

Did Lizzie Borden do it? We'll probably never know for sure. However, if dark forces had been conjured in the house, they may have inspired her to commit the ghastly deed. The devil once roamed here. He's waiting in the shadows of the Lizzie Borden B&B, patiently plotting a return.

CRIME PROFILE: SUE VICKERY

It's common for Lizbeth to watch who comes into Maplecroft and then she will follow them throughout the house.
—Sue Vickery, Lizzie Borden B&B and Maplecroft

When I first walked inside of Fall River's iconic murder house, the Lizzie Borden B&B, I was expecting to be underwhelmed. I wasn't. In fact, within the first few minutes of my first overnight stay in 2017, I spotted a shadow figure dart out of the dining room, and I connected deeply with Lizzie Borden's stepmother, Abby, in the John Morse room. I was in tears when I walked over to the scene of the crime.

Sue Vickery, a tour guide at the Lizzie Borden B&B, said my sensitivities were spot on. "Yes, it's a very common experience," she told me. "I've also been overcome with sadness on occasion in that room. I've had guests walk through that doorway and break out in tears."

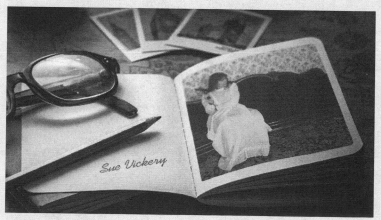

Vickery, who was featured twice on the Travel Channel's *Kindred Spirits* with Amy Bruni and Adam Berry, said the hauntings at the Lizzie Borden B&B live up to the building's national reputation. "The Bordens are very much still a presence here," she said. "I've spoken with Andrew, Abby, Lizzie, and occasionally Emma through the spirit box. I've witnessed black mist and white mist. I've had voices speak when no one is in the house. Footsteps are common. Doors open and close. I've been touched on numerous occasions as well."

When the owners of the Second Street murder house purchased Borden's later-in-life home called Maplecroft, Vickery invited me to check out the Queen Anne–style house, which had been closed to the public for years. After spending several sleepless nights at the extremely haunted bed and breakfast, I tentatively agreed to go to the house that was basically purchased with the Borden family's blood money.

At this point, I had no idea my visit to Maplecroft in July 2019 would rock my world and challenge my opinion of the woman who was accused of murdering her parents.

Borden moved into 306 French Street in 1893 with her sister, Emma, after being acquitted of the hatchet-job killings of her father and stepmother. The famous unsolved slaying has left a psychic imprint on the Second Street crime scene, but does ghostly energy linger in the house Borden inhabited until her death in 1927?

"Yes, she's here," Vickery told me when she let me into Maplecroft's side door. "She will greet you in the parlor."

Vickery believes that Borden, who opted for the name "Lizbeth" after the murders, continues to stick around in the afterlife in her more fashionable home located in Fall River's upscale Highlands neighborhood . . . and so does her sister, Emma.

"I didn't expect any activity at Maplecroft," Vickery explained as she gave me a tour of the property. "I was surprised to discover her here."

Vickery, who appeared on the 2019 episode of *Kindred Spirits*, which explored this historic home along with psychic Chip Coffey, said that people who are sensitive to the paranormal claim that Andrew Borden's youngest daughter will greet them in the downstairs parlor. "It's common for Lizbeth to watch who comes into Maplecroft, and then she will follow them throughout the house."

The spot where I sensed Borden the strongest was near the staircase on the first floor. Of course, this was where her body was kept. "She was not waked, and they held a funeral service in the parlor," Vickery explained. "Her death was kept secret from the public until she was buried."

As soon as Vickery and I walked into the first-floor room where her memorial was held, the sheet music that was played at her funeral service mysteriously blew off the piano stand. The song "My Ain Countrie" was significant to Borden. In fact, the lyrics to the Scottish folk song are etched into the mantel of her fireplace.

As this point of the tour, I heard what sounded like a dog approach me. I could clearly hear chains or a leash rattle, but there were no pets in the house. Of course, Borden had a fondness for Boston terriers and owned three of them. Her dogs, named Royal Nelson, Donald Stuart, and Laddie Miller, lived with Borden at Maplecroft. In 1913, she helped fund a fledgling rescue center for animals in Fall River. Based on my experience near the parlor, the spirits of Borden's pets continue to linger in their home.

Ghost dogs? Yep, Maplecroft has them.

While she hasn't encountered any spectral animals in the three-story structure, Vickery said that she had several paranormal experiences at the property during the restoration process. "As far as activity goes, I heard door slams while I was alone in the house and got touched on my leg while hanging a shower curtain," Vickery said. "I had a woman say 'hello' out loud, and no one was there. We heard someone walk across the upper floor while we sat downstairs in the parlor."

As Vickery and I were chatting, I clearly heard the word "mom" whispered in my ear. I quickly looked up, and there was a photo of Sarah Borden hanging on the wall. "I don't know why she would say 'mom'; perhaps she tried to contact her biological mother, Sarah," Vickery explained. "Lizbeth was very young when she died in 1863. However, Emma was eleven or twelve, and she was very close with her mother. If it wasn't Lizbeth who whispered in your ear, it could have been Emma."

Speaking of Borden's attempts to contact her deceased mother, Sarah, through a séance, Vickery said it was definitely possible that she tried to reach out to the other side because spiritualism was in vogue at the time. While Vickery can't prove the speculation, others from the paranormal community have validated the idea that séances were held at Maplecroft.

Vickery's psychic medium friend Glenn Teza was interviewed by the *Herald News* on March 5, 2018, and he strongly believes that either Lizbeth or Emma Borden, or possibly both sisters, attempted to make contact with the spirit realm.

In the newspaper article, Teza said he was "shocked" that Borden's later-in-life home was haunted. "There was a lot of activity," Teza told the *Herald News*. "I was really surprised. I didn't expect anything paranormal."

The psychic medium said he picked up on both of the Borden sisters in the house. "I did see Lizzie in the hallway in a deep purple satin dress," Teza told the newspaper. "She looked like she did when she was acquitted, but not as heavy. She was fairly young."

Teza also said that he encountered a psychic imprint on the top floor. "Upstairs in a small room on the third floor, thought to have been used for séances in Lizzie's time, Teza found two more spirits: an 'older gentleman' and a woman, both mediums," Teza told *Herald News* reporter Deborah Allard. "The gentleman, he said, 'stood up' and looked 'indignant' to have been interrupted."

After that initial baseline sweep with Teza, Vickery has been leading several public paranormal investigations at Maplecroft with her fellow Lizzie Borden B&B cohort, Deb Vickers. As I explored the house with the veteran tour guide, Vickery said that it shocked her that there was paranormal activity in the home's second-floor addition. She pointed out a few aspects to the side room, like an old-school servant bell pull system and a wall support designed for the elderly, that would suggest that Borden spent her twilight years in the more accessible addition built in 1909.

"While we have no proof, I believe she passed in this room," Vickery told me, pointing to the second-floor addition's design elements, which suggest it was built for someone with mobility issues. "You can feel her energy here," she added. "We believe she died in this room and continues to spend the most time here in the afterlife."

During the investigation featured on *Kindred Spirits*, Amy Bruni and Adam Berry had an intense spirit-box conversation with Lizbeth in the add-on bedroom located on the second floor. It was from this televised interaction that the house's staff surmised that Borden didn't want to be asked about the infamous double murder on Second Street. "This was her sanctuary," Vickery told me. "During our tours at Maplecroft, we don't mention the murders out of respect. She made it clear with the investigation on *Kindred Spirits* that she didn't want to be called to Second Street. This was her home. She doesn't want anything to do with what happened at the Lizzie Borden B&B."

When Vickery's fellow tour guide, Deb Vickers, was interviewed on *Kindred Spirits*, it was clear that both Vickery and Vickers make a concerted effort to respect Borden at Maplecroft. "Lizzie died in this house, and it's kind of sad. She was really lonely," Vickers said on *Kindred Spirits*. "She moved here to this house on the hill where she always wanted to live, but she was still ostracized by the community."

After guiding me down the stairs from the second-floor addition, Vickery led me to Maplecroft's basement. The tour guide and investigator said she has had several encounters with a male entity who has a history of being frisky with Maplecroft's female guests.

Vickery believes that the hands-on spirit that she's interacted with may have been the one who touched her leg in Borden's bathroom on the second floor. "I was hanging a shower curtain," Vickery explained on *Kindred Spirits*. "I felt like an electrical jolt on the back of my leg. You could feel fingers attached to the jolt."

It was initially believed that Borden touched Vickery in the bathroom. However, based on the electronic voice phenomena captured during the *Kindred Spirits* investigation, Lizbeth said that she "didn't do it."

Borden did have a chauffeur named Joseph Tetrault (pronounced Tatro). According to local lore, Emma didn't like him, and he was rumored to be a charming man who may have committed adultery in 1893. "Joseph Tetrault was fired in 1903, and Lizbeth rehired him in 1904," Vickery explained. "Some believe he was why Emma moved out in 1905."

Tetrault was popular with the ladies, and Vickery believes he's a flirt in the afterlife. "He's very touchy," Vickery said in the basement, adding that he likely camped out in the cellar. "He means well but has overstepped boundaries in the past."

Vickery said that she was surprised to discover that there was a male spirit in the house in addition to both Borden sisters. "We don't know who the man is, but we're guessing that it's Joseph Tetrault. He worked for her and I believe they were friends."

Based purely on my visit in July 2019, I would rank Maplecroft as one of the most haunted locations in New England. While I strongly believe the building is paranormally active, I got the message loud and clear from the spirits of this historic residence: respect them, and they will respect you in return. I definitely walked away from Borden's later-in-life home with a completely different perspective of the woman who was demonized during her trial by the media and then ostracized by the community. I also encountered a ghost dog for the first time during an investigation.

Thank you, Lizbeth.

Boston Strangler

On September 8, 1963, Evelyn Corbin, a fifty-eight-year-old divorcée, was found on her bed on Lafayette Street in Salem. She was half-naked with two silk stockings knotted around her neck. Albert DeSalvo, the self-professed Boston Strangler, confessed to the string of 1960s' killings that terrified the Boston area. However, new evidence suggests that the Corbin murder may have been a copycat crime.

From June 1962 through January 1964, there was a serial killer on the loose terrorizing women. Thirteen single women were killed and at least eleven of them were victims of the so-called Boston Strangler. While the police didn't see a connection with all thirteen slayings, the public did.

At all the crime scenes, the victims had been sexually attacked and were strangled by articles of their own clothing. There were no signs of forced entry. It's believed that all thirteen of the women voluntarily let the perpetrator into their homes.

The strangler's last victim, nineteen-year-old Mary Sullivan, was killed on January 4, 1964, on Charles Street in Boston's Beacon Hill. Sullivan's two roommates were working that day. She had the day off.

Sullivan's body was violated with a broom handle, and there were marks around her neck indicating that she was strangled by a nylon stocking. A pink-and-white floral scarf was tied in a bow to disguise the wounds. The Boston Strangler also left a card propped up next to the victim that said, "Happy New Year."

After Sullivan's murder, it took ten months until a suspect was apprehended. DeSalvo was identified after he tied up a woman and then sexually assaulted her. He then bolted from the scene, saying, "I'm sorry," as he left.

While there was no physical evidence to back up his claims, DeSalvo confessed to the murders. He was sentenced to life in prison in 1967. He soon escaped with two fellow inmates from Bridgewater State Hospital, which triggered a nationwide manhunt. He turned himself in and then transferred to a maximum-security prison in Walpole.

After being incarcerated for seven years, DeSalvo recanted his confession in 1973. He only admitted to the crimes because he wanted the fame associated with being the Boston Strangler, DeSalvo claimed. The following day, he was found stabbed to death in his cell. He was buried in the Puritan Lawn Memorial Park in Peabody.

The killer or killers were never identified.

Police investigators assigned to the Evelyn Corbin murder case have always believed that DeSalvo didn't strike in Salem. Inspector John Moran, a former police detective who recently passed, recounted his initial impressions at the Langdon Apartments on Lafayette Street in 1963.

Moran's first response when he entered the crime scene? "We've got another strangler here," he told *Salem News* reporter Tom Dalton in 2013.

"Corbin had breakfast with an elderly female tenant on the first floor that morning before going back to her apartment around 9:30 a.m., according to the Salem police files. That was the last time she was seen alive," reported Dalton. "When police entered the apartment, they found Corbin on a bed, half-naked, with two silk stockings knotted around her neck."

Moran, who retired in 1981 as a lieutenant, told Dalton that he was convinced that DeSalvo didn't murder Corbin. "I think it was a copycat, and there was more than one," Moran said. "Of course, DeSalvo went and confessed to all of the cases and how he got in. I never ever bought him on any of them."

The evidence that haunted Moran for years? It involved donuts. When he investigated how the murderer was able to break into the apartment, the detective found two donuts on the fire escape, "like somebody was going to climb in the window and didn't want to crush [them]," the detective recalled.

Moran then questioned a twenty-five-year-old man from Lynn. The suspect had stayed at a friend's apartment close to the crime scene and reportedly put a couple of donuts in his pocket, according to a witness, the morning of the murder. The suspect also left Salem the day after the slaying and mysteriously drove to Hudson, New York, with a sixteen-year-old girl in his car.

According to the *Salem News* article, Moran was never able to charge the Lynn man with Corbin's murder. DeSalvo confessed in

1964. In hindsight, the late, great Moran believed the two donuts found at the crime scene were enough to raise a few red flags.

DeSalvo was exhumed from his gravesite in Peabody to test his DNA. According to the forensic report, he did kill Mary Sullivan in Boston.

But what about Evelyn Corbin in Salem?

Boston Strangler's Haunt: Old Salem Jail

SALEM, MA—Salem's reportedly haunted correctional facility, which is believed to be the site of an estimated fifty hangings, has a long history of housing human monsters. Its lineup of usual suspects included DeSalvo for a short stint; hitman Joseph "The Animal" Barboza; former Mafia underboss Genaro Angiulo; and Brinks robber Joseph J. "Specs" O'Keefe.

Conditions in the old Salem Jail, which has oddly been refurbished into posh apartments, were notoriously horrific.

"It was a place that didn't have electricity or plumbing even in the 1960s and 1970s," said Tim Maguire from the Salem Night Tour. "Atrocities happened there, more so than executions, and they would kill each other in the prison because the conditions were so unbearable."

The granite-walled jail and Federal-style keeper's house opened in 1813 next to the Howard Street Cemetery, where Giles Corey was crushed to death in 1692. The building was expanded in 1884, at which time its signature gothic, Victorian, and mosque cupolas were placed on the roof. The building's addition was constructed with Rockport granite salvaged from St. Peter Street near the exact spot where Corey was pressed to death. Some believed the rocks used to build the jail were soaked with blood from the 1692 witch trial executions.

Almost 100 years later, conditions were so awful inside—inmates still had to use chamber pots for bathrooms—that a few prisoners successfully sued the county because of its inhumane living conditions. When it closed in 1991, after a 177-year run as a county jail, the Essex County Correctional Institute or old Salem Jail was considered the oldest active penitentiary in the United States.

"We have left the dungeon behind us," said Essex County sheriff Charles H. Reardon at a ribbon-cutting ceremony for the new facility in Middleton in the 1990s.

But did they really? For more than a decade, the 31,630-square-foot jail ominously stood vacant. The boarded-up structure became a popular hot spot for vandals, and its historic facade started to look like a scene pulled from a Stephen King novel. It was during the 1990s that the infamous correctional facility near the Howard Street Cemetery became the epicenter of Salem's ghost lore.

Based purely on aesthetics when it was vacant, the old Salem Jail looked haunted.

"Many locals would go inside the jail and try to retrieve artifacts left behind," said tour guide Sarah-Frankie Carter. "It was common for people to see shadow people inside and even outside on the grounds. It was an extremely active location, and people talked about feeling a heaviness in the air. The conditions were really bad there, so I'm not surprised."

The riots at the Old Salem Jail were legendary. In July 1980, six inmates turned the facility into a sewer after dumping waste buckets on the floors at the institution. When the prisoners were evacuated from the pre–Civil War facility in 1991, they "threw food, lit trash cans on fire, and threw urine-filled buckets throughout the jail," reported the *Salem Evening News*. One inmate wrote "We won" in toothpaste on a table in the prison's rectory. According to another newspaper report on February 21, 1991, the mess included "pizza boxes, clothing, and food thrown about the jail. Also, windows and televisions were smashed and several walls kicked in."

The building became a "magnet for vandals just one year after Essex County leaders vowed to give it to the city," reported the *Salem Evening News* on August 15, 1997. "The 185-year-old building had again been vandalized and some copper piping stolen from it."

It became a hangout for thrill-seeking locals during the late 1990s. "Kids have been getting in there, and it's become a party place," said Salem police captain Harold Blake in the 1997 newspaper report. "Someone's going to be liable if anything happens there, and I hope it doesn't fall on the city."

As far as spirits, people regularly heard whispers and "metal-like" sounds echoing throughout the structure when it was abandoned. There was also a residual haunting of what appeared to be a prisoner holding a candle and walking from room to room . . . on a floor that no longer existed and had collapsed years prior.

The jail grounds were extremely active, and several locals claimed to have seen shadow figures and full-bodied apparitions of former prisoners darting across the yard and heading toward the chain-link fence as if they were making their great escape in the afterlife. Civil War soldiers, who were imprisoned in the Old Salem

Jail, were seen wearing nineteenth-century clothing and moaning in agony from war-related punishments. In fact, several prisoners who spent time at the Essex County Correctional Institute said they shared a cell with long-gone inmates, or "residents" as they were called in the 1980s, from the Civil War era.

One explanation for the onslaught of so-called spectral evidence from the abandoned structure was that the living were reportedly coexisting with the dead. Yes, the jail had squatters. "People have been living there for nine years," said former public works director Stanley Bornstein in the October 15, 1999, edition of the *Salem Evening News*. "You patch one hole, they open another. Whatever you do, you're not going to keep people out of there. Somebody could easily be killed in there."

After the infamous penitentiary was turned into upscale condos and what was the sheriff's office became a popular St. Peter Street restaurant formerly called the Great Escape, A&B Burgers, and now Bit Bar Salem, the dark shadows from its past seem to have taken a break. Perhaps their torturous sentence behind bars extended after death, and once the cell blocks were removed and the space was transformed, the correctional facility's invisible prisoners were finally set free. Or the Old Salem Jail's squatters—both the living and their spirited roommates—found a new home.

The granite-walled jail and Federal-style keeper's house opened in 1813 next to the Howard Street Cemetery, where Giles Corey was crushed to death during the witch-trials hysteria in 1692. The jail was expanded in 1885 when two octagonal cupolas were constructed. Magician Harry Houdini staged an escape in 1906.

Visitors to Bit Bar Salem's restaurant and arcade can get a ringside seat to Salem's most haunted cemetery. Opened next to the old Salem Jail, the spooky graveyard on a hill is the final resting spot for seafarer Benjamin Ropes, who was buried there on August 5, 1801. Cause of death? Ropes was fatally crushed while launching the historic ship *Belisarius*'s top mast. Oddly, a large percentage of those buried in the Howard Street Cemetery had a fate similar to Giles Corey, the only witch trial victim who suffered the "peine forte et dure" form of execution. Yep, a large percentage of those buried there were accidentally or purposefully crushed.

"We did some research with the city, and we found that a high number of people buried in the Howard Street Cemetery, around fifteen percent, were crushed to death," explained Maguire. "It's so interesting because that was the site where Giles Corey was crushed to death during the witch trials."

The Salem Night Tour owner rattled off a series of bizarre "accidents" of those buried at the Howard Street Cemetery. "For example, the floor of the jail collapsed and killed ten prisoners," he said. "A high number of people buried there were crushed to death because of various accidents."

Maguire was a featured player on the History Channel 2's documentary focusing on a handful of Salem's alleged haunts. The evidence he unveiled on the show, specifically a photo taken at the Howard Street Cemetery, was shocking. The picture looked like a crowd of Puritan-era revelers gathered in a lynch mob sort of way around what is believed to be the exact spot where Corey was stripped naked, placed under a wooden board, and crushed to death over a two-day period in 1692.

"Someone on my tour took a photo of the cemetery," Maguire said on the History Channel. "By the end of the tour, that person came forward to share the photo he took. Definitely not what we were looking at. There seem to be figures of people standing over someone. Most people who feel like they found the spirit of Giles Corey or have seen his apparition, they think it's a reminder of what we have done to him there."

Maguire told me that he rarely gives daytime tours. However, a Christian-based group requested an earlier time slot one day, and they snapped the infamous picture. "In the photo, you see what looks like flames in the background, and you can make out a couple of faces in the photo," he said, convinced he captured something paranormal. "When we were standing there, it was a nice, clear, sunny day."

Over the years, Maguire said he's heard of multiple Corey sightings. "People often see an old man go around a tree there. It seems to be the spirit of Giles Corey," he said, adding that the burial ground's proximity to the Old Salem Jail adds to its negative energy. "What's interesting about the Howard Street Cemetery is that it was built to accommodate inmate atrocities. It was the only coed jail in the country. Women were on one side, men on the other, and children in the middle. There was a four-year-old boy who served a two-month sentence for breaking something."

It's common for visitors to report heart palpitations or a sensation of a heavy weight being placed on their upper body, just like the stubborn landowner who had rocks placed on his chest. It's also the norm for Salemites to mention Corey's curse.

"All of the Essex County sheriffs who overlooked that property eventually died of a heart-related ailment," said Maguire. "Robert Cahill (author of *Haunted Happenings* and sheriff who lived to seventy) was a firm believer in the curse. He had a bizarre blood ailment they couldn't diagnose. It's believed that Corey cursed the city and the sheriff in blood . . . and we have proof."

And if someone sees his apparition? Salem allegedly burns.

"My friend and I were exploring the Howard Street Cemetery," recalled Sarah-Frankie Carter on the History Channel. "There was a very creepy feeling as we got closer and closer to the spot where Giles Corey was actually pressed to death. My friend wiggled through a fence to see if she could get a closer look at the jail, and I heard her scream. She said she saw a man standing at the top of the stairs. We both had a really bad feeling."

Carter echoed the legend that if the "skeleton of Corey's ghost in tattered old clothes" appears, something horrible will happen to the city. "They say if you see Giles Corey, Salem burns. And if he speaks to you, you die," she said, adding that Salem did, in fact, go up in flames after her Corey sighting. "I was listening to my local college radio station, and they said there were fires in Salem. Needless to say, I don't go to that part of Salem anymore, especially at night. I don't think he gives you many chances."

Locals believe in Corey's curse. In fact, author Nathaniel Hawthorne claimed that the apparition "of the wizard appears as a precursor to some great calamity impending over the community."

According to several accounts, Corey's spirit was spotted near the Howard Street Cemetery days before the Great Fire of 1914 that completely annihilated one-third of the city. Ironically, the inferno began in Gallows Hill, where nineteen innocents were hanged, and the conflagration destroyed one-third of Salem. "Before the Great Fire of 1914, there were almost three hundred accounts of local Salemites who had gone to the sheriff's office and reported this old man in raggedy clothes that they tried to help and then who vanished," confirmed Maguire, adding that he doesn't have solid proof of the lore. "They put enough stock into these accounts that the sheriff put deputies around the Howard Street Cemetery. They actually watched that cemetery for six or seven hours, and when they had left, the Great Fire happened about a half hour after."

Apparently, Corey's spirit continues to hold the city of Salem accountable.

Dr. George Parkman

One of the most heinous crimes from Boston's past centers on Dr. George Parkman, who was beaten and dismembered in a Harvard Medical College laboratory in 1849. Based on a bizarre plumbing accident that occurred on November 23, 1999, exactly 150 years after Parkman's macabre murder, his spirit is rumored to haunt the house that bears his family name. It faces the Boston Common and is located at 33 Beacon Street. Also, the Parkman Bandstand, located in the center of the public park and erected posthumously after the "crime of the century," stands as a solemn reminder of one of the most talked-about trials of the 1800s.

It's a tale of a four hundred–dollar loan turned deadly.

Hailing from one of the most prominent families in Boston, Parkman was a retired doctor who became a landlord and money lender in the early 1800s. Nicknamed "Old Chin," Parkman befriended one of his clients, John White Webster, who was a professor of chemistry and geology at Harvard Medical College. Incidentally, the Parkman family donated a large sum of money to fund Harvard's medical school, which was formerly located near the Massachusetts General Hospital.

Webster borrowed four hundred dollars from Parkman, who was reported missing days following an attempt to collect his money. Bostonians were on the hunt for the missing landlord, and police printed twenty-eight thousand missing-person fliers. After a sensational trial and Webster's eventual confession, the press had a field day spitting out "Harvard Professor and Murderer" headlines guaranteed to captivate the city. On August 30, 1850, the professor was hanged at the gallows in Boston Common.

How did Webster murder Parkman? After an unexpected collections call at Webster's laboratory, the professor took his walking stick and clubbed Parkman in the head during a momentary fit of rage. Panicked, Webster reportedly chopped up the body into pieces and threw the remains into the privy, also known as a toilet.

In his confession, Webster claimed that it was an act of self-defense. He said that Parkman "was speaking and gesticulating in the most violent and menacing manner" about the loan. In response, Webster "seized whatever thing was handiest—it was a stick of wood—and dealt him an instantaneous blow with all the force that passion could give it. It was on the side of his head, and there was nothing to break the force of the blow. He instantly fell upon the pavement. There was no second blow. He did not move."

During the trial, a police officer testified that Parkman's torso was found in a bloodstained tea chest, which was displayed to the court. Webster also allegedly burned Parkman's bones, including his jawbone complete with false teeth, in the furnace. The officer also said that it was possible to fit the victim's remaining body parts in the toilet, but the torso wouldn't fit.

So, when Parkman's former home on Beacon Street was destroyed in a plumbing accident in 1999, historians and paranormal experts weren't surprised. Just days before the house was due to host the mayor of Boston, a cistern was broken in a third-floor toilet at the Parkman House and the tank overflowed. "The water was gushing everywhere. It was the worst possible scenario. The toilet on the third floor was broken, and the water kept running and running and running, and the water leaked down to the second floor and then the first floor, so there was quite a bit of damage," said Cecily Foster, who oversaw the Parkman House and was director of tourism, in a *Boston Globe* article. "Maybe the ghost of Dr. Parkman came to visit last night."

Perhaps he did. The late Jim McCabe, who was a noted ghost lore expert and owner of New England Ghost Tours, explained why Parkman may have returned to his Beacon Hill brownstone. "The old Yankees may have been strange in certain ways, but they kept the old buildings, which has made it attractive to many visitors— even ghosts," McCabe told the *Boston Globe*. "Spirits are attracted to the places they lived in. I think what attracts ghosts up here is that you don't tear down the buildings."

Charles Dickens, who was intrigued by the infamous murder, paid a visit to Webster's laboratory eighteen years after the trial. His response to the murder scene? The *Christmas Carol* and *Great Expectations* author said that "the room smelled as if the body was there." Based on the freakish plumbing disaster marking the anniversary of Parkman's death, Dickens should have checked out the murdered doctor's palatial Beacon Hill estate.

Yes, fact is stranger than fiction.

PARKMAN'S HAUNT: HARVARD UNIVERSITY

CAMBRIDGE, MA—In 2014, I was interviewed by my friend Sarah Sweeney for the *Harvard Gazette* about the alleged hauntings lingering at the prestigious Ivy League college in Cambridge. "In my opinion, Memorial Hall is Harvard's most haunted," I told Sweeney. "Spirits have been seen looking out the windows and even walking the lawns outside the hall."

The article was published months after I was given an impromptu tour of the Annenberg dining complex within Memorial Hall. My first impression during the walkthrough? It looks like the Great Hall featured in the Harry Potter films. The structure, modelled after Christ Church in Oxford, features magnificent stained-glass windows by John La Farge, known for his work at Trinity Church in Boston, and glass from Tiffany's founder, Louis Comfort Tiffany.

While looking from the upper level to the dining hall, I swear I spotted what looked like a young man trying to get my attention from across the hall. He was wearing period garb and disappeared after a second glance. I was told later that the spot where I saw the full-bodied apparition is Annenberg Hall's most paranormally active area.

One employee, who works in the historic building, believes there's an inexplicable energy, or a supernatural imprint, left on the space. "Sometimes it feels like somebody or something walks by, and there's nobody there," he said. "It's like when somebody walks by and you feel the air move. Sometimes late at night, it feels like there is somebody standing behind you. It's so bizarre."

The source, who wishes to remain anonymous, said the area directly above Annenberg Hall's dining area is the building's most-active spot for alleged paranormal activity. "I like to think it was a former student, possibly one of the Civil War soldiers the building was built for," he said. "Because Annenberg Hall has always been a dining hall, it could be a chef or somebody who is in between worlds and is transitioning. I think the spirit is stuck and doesn't know which way to go," he said, adding that his friend who is a spiritualist confirmed that Memorial Hall is indeed haunted.

For several years, I produced a ghost tour called Cambridge Haunts, and we had repeated sightings and hard-to-explain photos shot in the area believed to be Cambridge's haunted corridor. All the guides on the ghost walk agreed Memorial Hall was the most active location on the tour. "The building is electric, and you can feel the energy when you're entering the pub," confirmed Hank Fay, a tour guide with Cambridge Haunts and local musician who regularly performed at the campus haunt. "When we're loading equipment in the area behind Queen's Head, the back of my hair stands up. There's definitely something strange going on in that building."

Another former tour guide, Rob Oftring, said he had an emotional connection with one of the tour's alleged spirits. The site is literally across the street from Memorial Hall. "Sam, I swear I saw Bertha standing in the yard on Kirkland Street," he told me, adding that he felt like the spirit had something to tell him.

Who's Bertha? According to published reports, she was believed to have been murdered in a house no longer standing on Kirkland Street across from Harvard's Memorial Hall. Human bones were found on the property, but the victim was never identified.

Yes, Cambridge had its own version of *The Amityville Horror* known as the "Kirkland Street Nightmare." The Treadwell-Sparks House located at 21 Kirkland Street was originally built in 1838 and was moved from Quincy Street to its current location in 1968. However, the house that stood there before had a haunted history that made headlines in the *Boston Daily Globe* on April 8, 1878.

Over a fifteen-year span, tenants at the original house would come and go without giving any explanation. There were reports of disembodied voices, and after a series of revolving-door dwellers, the double-decker was abandoned for years because of its "haunted house" reputation. College students threw rocks through the windows, and stressed-out Harvard kids would squat at the dilapidated house for a spooky night out. In 1878, a man described as Mr. Marsh and his family rented the homestead for fifteen dollars a month and shrugged off the rumors that the house was haunted.

Soon, Marsh started hearing his name called out by an evil disembodied voice. He also watched in horror as the handle of his door slowly turned and opened when no one, at least among the living, was in the room. After close encounters with an unseen force, the man organized a Victorian-style séance. During the spiritual intervention, Marsh's wife allegedly became possessed by the so-called spirit haunting the house. Mrs. Marsh described in detail the story of an orphan girl who was forcibly taken into the home by a carriage where she was, according to the report, "foully dealt with, murdered and buried in the cellar below the house." During the séance, the spirit said her name was Bertha.

After a few months without paranormal activity, the house's freaked-out tenants started hearing odd noises in the home and up the stairs. They also heard glass shattering in the kitchen, yet nothing was broken. The maid claimed she heard "terrible noises" at night and said the furniture in the room was pushed by invisible hands. She also recalled hearing bloodcurdling shrieks and cries from a female voice.

After the initial article called "The Spook Roost" appeared in the *Globe*, former residents recalled seeing a full-bodied apparition of a young girl. They recounted objects, like plates on the kitchen table, moving when no one was there. Hundreds of curious spectators gathered around the Kirkland Street house at night while Mr. Marsh dug in the cellar to find the remains of the supposedly murdered girl known as Bertha.

Bones were found in the basement. However, a former tenant claimed that he would bury slaughtered animal bones in the cellar. Investigators couldn't tell if the remains were human or animal. In 1878, the police didn't have the forensic and DNA tools investigators use today.

The Marshes, after undergoing public scrutiny because of the reports in the *Globe*, stopped talking to the press and demanded privacy. After several years, they fled the haunted house on Kirkland Street, and it was eventually demolished.

A former maid, Mary Nolan, confirmed the alleged haunting to the *Globe*. "Often, I heard the carriage drive up, stop, and then go on again. Why, that was quite common. We would hear the sound of wheels, the hoofs of the horses, and sometimes the crack of the whip, but nothing could be seen. I wouldn't live in that house again for $1,000," Nolan said. "It was enough to frighten people to death."

The late Reverend Peter Gomes, a prominent Harvard theologian and author who lived in the Treadwell-Sparks House until his passing, commented about the ghost lore surrounding Divinity Hall. The Kirkland Street house is near Harvard Divinity. "It was said that if you heard strange noises by the chapel or saw someone there you didn't recognize, it was probably a ghost," Gomes said, adding that the spirits were believed to be "benign, doubtless Unitarian, rational ghosts." Gomes never commented on the female spirit allegedly haunting his home on Kirkland Street.

William James—a Harvard luminary and founder of the American Society for Psychical Research, which is one of the oldest organizations exploring the paranormal—lived at 95 Irving Street, which is a stone's throw from the Kirkland Street haunt. His first essay for the society was about a girl who mysteriously vanished from her home in Enfield, New Hampshire. James investigated the haunting premonitions of Nellie Titus, who allegedly predicted how the sixteen-year-old died on Halloween in the late 1800s. According to the essay, Titus strongly believed that the girl drowned near a Shaker-style bridge in Enfield. Her body was found, but the case continues to be a mystery.

The dead girl's name? Bertha Huse.

Based on my firsthand experience, history and mystery lurk in just about every crimson corner at Cambridge's prestigious Ivy League. Harvard University is full of secrets, and its ghost lore reflects this centuries-old legacy of dead presidents and long-gone intelligentsia. Spine-chilling tales of unexplained sounds, phantom knocking, and full-bodied apparitions have become a rite of passage for the uninitiated, college-bound progeny adapting to life in one of the Hogwarts-style halls scattered throughout Harvard Yard.

Elizabeth Tucker, a professor of English at Binghamton University and author of *Haunted Halls: Ghostlore of American College Campuses*, said that collegiate ghost stories are morality plays for the modern era. "They educate freshmen about how to live well in college," she explained in a 2007 interview, adding that the cautionary tales serve as spooky metaphors of fear, disorder, and insanity. They also reflect students' interest in their college's historical legacy. Yep, campus ghost lore is a paranormal pep rally of sorts. "You don't find ghost stories at schools without a sense of pride," Tucker continued. "School spirits reflect school spirit."

The difference between Harvard's specters and other run-of-the-mill ghosts haunting universities throughout the country? Their spirits are wicked smart. Harvard's Massachusetts Hall has one respectable-looking student who returns every fall claiming to be a member of the class of 1914. Apparently, the residual apparition of Holbrook Smith never got the memo that he was kicked out of the Ivy League almost a century ago. There's also a Civil War–era apparition that allegedly haunts Memorial Hall. In 1929, a proctor reported seeing a man who wasn't enrolled in the class show up with a blue book in hand. The school spirit was known as the Memorial Hall ghost, and the "left behind" (a spirit that doesn't know he's dead) kept returning to class to finish the test—even though he died long ago.

Holden Chapel, which was used as the first cadaver room when the college hosted the Harvard Medical College, is rumored to be teeming with ghosts from its past. Built in 1744, the

Colonial-style building was the spiritual gathering place as well as a secular lecture hall for Harvard students until 1772. The chapel housed 160 soldiers from 1775 to 1776 in the days leading up to the American Revolution. It later became the hub of Harvard's burgeoning medical school, established in 1783 by John Warren, and served for half a century as a morgue for students in training.

One legend alludes to Holden Chapel's macabre medical history. According to the late William C. "Burriss" Young, who lived in nearby Mass Hall as an assistant dean of freshmen, there's a female spirit who returns to Holden Chapel every year "around the first snowstorm."

Her name? Pickham.

According to Young, she was "a woman who was riding with her fiancé in a sleigh through the square when their horse slipped on the ice and their sleigh flipped over. Her fiancé broke his neck and died in her arms." According to the legend, he was buried at the Old Burying Ground, but "when she returned to visit the grave, the body had been dug up and stolen."

Back in the day, resurrection men—or grave robbers—would keep careful track of who died and where they were buried. When there was an opportunity to sell a body to a medical school, the resurrection man would go and dig up someone recently deceased. It was common practice for people like Ephraim Littlefield, who was a janitor at the Harvard Medical School and rumored to be a grave robber, to retrieve a dead body when the medical school's stock of cadavers was getting low.

The female spirit that allegedly haunts Holden Chapel "became convinced that her husband's body was in Holden Chapel, which housed the dissecting labs at that time," continued Young. "Every year, at the first snowstorm, she would escape from her family's house in New Bedford and try to break into Holden Chapel and would have to be physically restrained from entering. She's still spotted from time to time," Young told the *Crimson* in 1997. "And if you ever see her, and you observe carefully, you'll notice that she doesn't leave any footprints in the snow."

The medical school moved in the 1800s from Harvard Yard to Boston, where one of its famous alums, Dr. John White Webster, was accused of what was called the crime of the century: the murder of Dr. George Parkman. It's likely that Webster and Parkman made their first contact at Holden Chapel in the early nineteenth century.

With such a macabre legacy, Holden Chapel today looks like a throwback to Harvard's days of yore. For most of the twentieth century, it hosted the Harvard Glee Club and later the Radcliffe Choral Society. The chapel was renovated in 1999, and archaeologists discovered human remains in the building's basement. "My first thought was 'Oooohh, an old Harvard murder,'" said Associate Professor of Anthropology Carole A. S. Mandryk in a 1999 *Crimson* interview. "They're definitely human bones." According to the report, workers found several sawed-open skeletons, broken scientific glassware, and test tubes strewn among the remains. "Between 1782 and 1850, part of the basement was used as an anatomy and dissection lecture hall for the Medical School," wrote the *Crimson*. "Some of the bones have metal pieces sticking out of them, as if someone was trying to construct a skeleton," Mandryk added.

Remember the wailing female spirit known as Pickham who returns to Holden Chapel during the first snowstorm? She hasn't been spotted since the building's renovations. It's possible that she was right, and her husband's remains were buried in the basement. Perhaps Pickham finally got some postmortem closure when the bones were unearthed and removed from Holden Chapel.

Hannah Duston

Lizzie Borden is the usual suspect when one mentions "hatchet murders" in Massachusetts. However, there was one woman who took an ax and killed her Native American captors. She was kidnapped during an incendiary raid on March 15, 1697, in Haverhill, Massachusetts. Six homes were burned during the attack, and at least thirty-nine people were killed or captured.

Hannah Duston, a controversial figure in local history, was snatched from her home along with her newborn daughter, Martha, and Mary Neff, who served as her midwife. According to the legend, Duston snapped after her newborn baby was killed by the Abenaki tribe. Soliciting the help of fourteen-year-old Samuel Lennardson, she retaliated and ultimately killed and scalped ten of the sleeping natives with a hatchet. Only one woman and a young man survived the woman's postpartum wrath.

Duston was canonized when she returned to Haverhill. However, not everybody views her as a Colonial-era heroine. Looking at the case with a modern lens, her revenge-killing spree leaves historians like Peter Muise uneasy. "I hope that I don't come across looking like I support white people killing Native Americans," Muise told me, "because I don't."

The *Legends and Lore of the North Shore* author said that he was equally intrigued and horrified by the stories that he was told about Duston in the 1970s, when his Boy Scout troop visited the Buttonwoods Museum in his hometown of Haverhill. "We were shown some artifacts associated with Hannah Duston, and I seem to remember even seeing her hatchet," he recalled. "As kids, we were taught that she was a heroine because she escaped from the natives who had kidnapped her after burning the town. Of course, she was always kind of a scary heroine because we also knew that she killed the natives while they slept and scalped them."

One horrifying detail that tugged on Muise's heartstrings involved the death of Duston's six-day-old daughter. "One of the Abenaki took Hannah's baby and smashed it against a tree as they left Haverhill with the captives," Muise told me. "As a kid, I was told this was because the infant wouldn't stop crying, but I don't know if that's true. The killing of her baby apparently is true, though, and it's a very gruesome detail."

As he matured, Muise said that he started to question Duston's motivation. Was she a heroine or just an unwitting soldier in an imperialist war? "As an adult, I can also see Hannah Duston as someone caught up in a larger political situation," he said. "The Abenaki who kidnapped her were allies of the French, who were at the time battling with England for control over North America. The attack on Haverhill was just a small part of what was called King William's War."

While "two wrongs don't make a right," Muise also viewed Duston as a traumatized mother who avenged the death of her child. "This doesn't make what she did right but helps make her motive clearer," he said. "However, she caused other mothers to grieve when she killed and scalped her kidnappers. It's just a grim and bloody story."

Another gruesome detail is that Duston was paid for the scalps of the men, women, and children that she slaughtered on the island in the Merrimack in what is now Boscawen, New Hampshire. It's where she was held prisoner by the Pennacook tribe. "The government of Massachusetts paid a bounty for Native American scalps earlier in the 1690s, but by 1697 they had repealed that law," Muise explained. "After hearing Hannah's story, they made an exception and gave her a reward of twenty-five pounds."

Muise said there are several memorial statues commemorating Duston's retaliatory killings. However, he's only seen the bronze statue erected in Haverhill's Grand Army Park, which features the controversial heroine holding a tomahawk and wearing only one shoe. "It's definitely scary," he told me. "She's pointing and brandishing her hatchet, ready to kill. Around the base of the statue are four plaques that illustrate her story."

As for the legends and lore associated with Duston, Muise said there was one tale featured in Eva Speare's book called *New Hampshire Folk Tales*. Duston was helped by a fairy named Tsienneto according to the story published in 1932. "Tsienneto supposedly lived in Beaver Lake in Derry, and she took pity on Hannah Duston when she and her captors stopped by the lake on their journey north," Muise said. "According to the legend, the Pennacook fell asleep because Tsienneto cast a spell on them. This is why they didn't wake up while they were being killed. The fairy also helped

Hannah, Mary Neff, and Samuel Lennardson get back to Haverhill in a stolen canoe."

Muise said he was baffled by this made-up tall tale. "Why would a native fairy help an English settler kill local indigenous people? It's always puzzled me."

DUSTON'S HAUNT: HILLDALE CEMETERY

HAVERHILL, MA—Based purely on its eerie aesthetic, Hilldale Cemetery in Haverhill should be haunted. It has all of the telltale signs: Civil War–era soldiers buried in a mass grave, desecrated headstones thanks to years of neglect, a series of unmarked plots where Haverhill's paupers were dumped, and urban legends involving all sorts of tales of the macabre, including a larger-than-usual tree believed to be used for hangings.

It's also a stone's throw from where victim-turned-killer Hannah Duston was believed to be kidnapped by the Abenaki tribe from Quebec during King William's War in 1697. Armed with a hatchet, Duston killed and then scalped her captors, which included men, women, and children.

Some believe there's an "aura of disaster" associated with the Native American attacks in Haverhill. In fact, sensitives to the paranormal can sense a lingering tension that has somehow psychically imprinted itself into the land at Hilldale Cemetery.

According to my tour guide, Thomas Spitalere, it's been an uphill battle trying to return this historic cemetery to its original glory. "Over there was a portal that we had to close," he said, talking about an area that has an unusually high level of energy that serves as a doorway to another dimension.

Spitalere, president of the cemetery's board of trustees, told me that he's encountered an onslaught of paranormal phenomena with his group of investigators called Essex County Ghost Project. There's a lady in white who reportedly rushes up to people in the cemetery. According to several psychics, she's mourning the loss of her soldier boyfriend. "She's wearing what looks like an old-school wedding dress," Spitalere said, adding that perhaps the ghostly lady continues to search for her mortally wounded love in the afterlife. "And over there we uncovered shadow figures," he said, pointing to an area near what has been divined as the hanging tree. "Near Soldier's Hill we have a photo of what looks like a head coming out of the ground."

The historian directed me to what he jokingly calls his "office," which happens to be the trunk of his car. He whipped out a binder of research and paranormal photos, including a picture of a soldier's grave, and, yes, there appears to be a disembodied head emerging in front of the commemorative marker.

When Spitalere's team researched the backstory of the soldier spirit, they learned that the floating head emerged in front of Henry J. White's gravestone. Spitalere said the man had an illustrious career as a drummer during the Civil War and even taught young soldiers the art of various drum rolls. The syncopated rhythms from the instrument—like "attack now" or "retreat"—reflected military orders during battle because it was difficult for the officers to understand verbal commands amid the noise and chaos of combat.

However, not all the spirits in Hilldale Cemetery are positive manifestations.

"We also have another lady who plays hide-and-seek with us," Spitalere said, adding that the entity wears Victorian-era garb and was more nefarious compared to the other female spirit in the wedding dress. "Over on what we call 'hangman's hill,' we had a few nasty things up there."

If Spitalere's account sounds like a cavalcade of fearsome phantoms pulled from the imagination of author H. P. Lovecraft, then it should be no surprise that the horror writer's friend and his first publisher is actually buried at Hilldale Cemetery. Yep, Charles W. "Tryout" Smith was interred down a path leading to what looks like a crevasse caused by the burial ground's glacial formations. A commemorative headstone honoring Smith's legacy in Haverhill was dedicated in September 2018.

For Spitalere, Hilldale is a historical goldmine of information from the Civil War era to the 1980s. Hilldale Cemetery was founded in 1859, and it's a garden-style burial ground with naturally steep hills caused by glaciers. "I call cemeteries outdoor museums," he told me. "Every gravestone has a story to tell."

In 2008, Spitalere was asked by Essex Heritage to catalog old cemeteries, and he eventually was tapped to be the volunteer director of the privately owned Hilldale. Apparently, all the previous trustees resigned. He said that the burial ground's historical significance is unparalleled and rattled off the shockingly large amount of skeletal remains in the cemetery, which includes at least four hundred Civil War veterans and countless pauper graves.

"There's around 4,820," he told WHAV radio in May 2017. "That's what we have in the book, but we have now located names on stones that aren't in the book. So, once this project is done—the cleaning—we're going to go stone to stone, row to row, and recatalog the cemetery."

Five years ago, the cemetery made headlines and not in a good way. Locals started to complain about its condition, and Spitalere had to literally explain the hurdles he faced to Haverhill's mayor. In addition to maintaining the yard, he had to combat severe vandalism "including several fires that were intentionally set, damaged gravestones, fenceposts that were spray-painted, toppled headstones, and trespassing by riders of dirt bikes and other recreational vehicles," reported an article in the *Eagle-Tribune* on August 13, 2013.

Since taking over, Spitalere said at least 50 percent of the gravestones at Hilldale Cemetery have been reclaimed. He also explained that the cemetery was comprised of at least twenty acres in the nineteenth century and is the result of a "terminal moraine," or a geological formation consisting of debris pushed forward by a glacier. The aesthetic is a truly unique landscape consisting of peaks and valleys and what is known as a "kame," or a moundlike hill of sand and gravel.

Caitlyn Pellerin, an empath and Spitalere's fiancée, talked about the spirits she's connected with at the burial ground. She's also channeled a few spirits during investigations, including two not-so-nice children entities near the potter's field, which is a dead man's dumping ground for paupers.

"Two of them are kids and two of them are not," the Essex County Ghost Project cofounder said, referencing the possibility of an entity manifesting as a child with at least two encounters she's had at Hilldale.

Both Pellerin and Spitalere said the burial ground "hasn't been investigated to death" and is a fairly untapped location for paranormal investigators. However, Spitalere warned that the grounds are private, and ghost hunters need permission to access what he believes is the most haunted cemetery in Massachusetts.

He also believes that the large percentage of unkempt and desecrated graves continues to leave a few spirits unhinged in the afterlife. "I had one team member spot a shadow figure wearing a sailor's hat over there," he said, pointing to one of the rolling hills. "When they went over to investigate, they lifted up the gravestone and put it back in place. We haven't seen that particular shadow figure since that episode."

Spitalere told me that his sensitivity to the paranormal has heightened during his tenure at Hilldale Cemetery. "I've channeled a World War II soldier, and I said stuff I will not repeat," he told me. "I also connected with a spirit of a soldier who had his leg blown off by a cannon."

When asked why a cemetery would be haunted, Spitalere gave a simple answer to a complex question. "Some spirits just don't want to leave the cemetery," he said. "Why do objects get haunted? Some people just don't know how to let go."

Pirates of Boston

Move over, witches. The most vilified group among the Colonial-era finger pointers were, in fact, the swashbuckling, "argh matey" set. Yep, pirates were arguably the most hated outsiders to ruffle the feathers of the notoriously intolerant settlers who fled to the new land seeking religious freedom.

Cindy Vallar, editor of the *Pirates and Privateers* newsletter, said early Bostonians demonized piracy more than the inhabitants of other cities, such as New York and Newport, Rhode Island, who treated their pirate visitors like rock stars. "The Puritan influence played a key role in Boston's history, and men like the Reverend Cotton Mather frequently preached on the evils of piracy. His sphere of influence was particularly strong and widespread," Vallar explained. "The colonial governors of Boston and Massachusetts were less tolerant of such crime."

Vallar, the Texas-based author of *Scottish Thistle*, told me that she noticed a clear negative bias toward the city's pirate interlopers. "Other places in the colonies didn't always see pirates in this same vein. They provided goods not available because of the Navigation Acts, and they provided a service—protection—in some places because England couldn't defend all her possessions. Politics also played a role in whether they were demonized or treated like rock stars."

In fact, Boston's pirates were hanged and displayed in crude contraptions known as gibbet cages on Nix's Mate and Bird Island in Boston Harbor. Vallar said the pirates were first hanged in what was then called Hudson's Point, which is in the general vicinity of Commercial and Charter Streets in Boston's North End. "On the day of their hanging, they were escorted by boat to Hudson's Point. That's where they were hanged on gallows in the mud flats," Vallar said. "English tradition was that since the courts fell under admiralty law, the corpses had to be washed by three tides before they could be disposed of. John Quelch and his men were the first to be tried in Boston," she continued, adding that earlier pirates were transported to London because vice-admiralty courts didn't exist before 1701.

Out of the handful of pirates tried in Boston, Vallar said three come to mind. "Captain William Kidd is probably the best known. Boston is where he was arrested on charges of murder and piracy. He was imprisoned here until he was transported to London to stand trial."

Vallar continued, "The second pirate is John Quelch. He's not well-known, but he was the first pirate to be tried in an admiralty court outside of England. The third pirate is William Fly, who refused to repent for his crimes—one of the few pirates not swayed by the Reverend Cotton Mather, or any minister, on the need to atone for his sins before dancing the 'hempen jig,' or hanging."

In addition to the possibly true lore associated with William Fly on Nix's Mate, one legend is associated with an unmarked grave at the rear of King's Chapel Burying Ground on Tremont Street. People claim to hear the raucous laughter of a pirate echoing throughout the cemetery. Although the gravestone has no name, many believe it's the final resting place of the infamous pirate Captain Kidd.

According to Vallar, it's not. While the salty dog was definitely arrested in Boston in 1701 and was hanged and buried in England, little proof exists to either support or disprove the idea that he haunts the historic burying ground.

Why would local legend embrace this historically inaccurate ghost story? Vallar said revisionism is commonplace when it comes to pirates. "I think word of mouth plays a key role. It's kind of like the whisper down the lane. One person tells the story, but the next tweaks it, and the teller after that does the same until the original version and the revised version no longer resemble each other. It's what makes good storytelling."

Vallar said she hadn't encountered any good ghost stories while debunking misinformation associated with Boston's buccaneers. "My readers are more interested in the pirates while they were alive rather than after they died," she joked.

For the record, there may be a kernel of truth associated with the King's Chapel legend. Yes, a lesser-known pirate was buried at King's Chapel Burying Ground. The body of John Lambert, a man executed for piracy, was confiscated and moved by his prominent Salem family and interred in an unmarked grave next to his deceased wife and son.

Perhaps Lambert is King's Chapel Burying Ground's pirate ghost? Shiver me timbers.

PIRATES' HAUNT: NIX'S MATE

BOSTON HARBOR, MA—Boston Harbor's smallest island is arguably its most mysterious. On Nix's Mate, reports have been made of a pirate specter known as William Fly, who was executed by hanging in the 1700s after apparently tying his own noose. Sailors who pass by the tiny, off-limits Nix's Mate claim to hear bloodcurdling screams and maniacal laughter on the island, which was once used to showcase accused pirates such as Fly in a crude contraption known as a gibbet cage.

Cindy Vallar, editor of *Pirates and Privateers*, said Nix's Mate, along with the long-gone Bird Island, played a pivotal role in Boston's "argh matey" history. But the truth behind the eroded island's legend continues to be a mystery. "I don't know a lot about Nix's Mate," Vallar remarked. "Mostly I've come across it when researching pirate executions. The most famous pirate to hang here was William Fly. The island may have been named for a captain who was murdered by one of his men and later hanged here, or Nix may have been a pirate himself."

Marked by a black-and-white stucco-covered day beacon mounted on a stone platform, Nix's Mate is a dangerous rocky shoal near the convergence of three major channels in Boston Harbor. Its central location was crucial to the Puritans when they were looking to ward off potential pirates. "If a pirate was made an example of, his gibbeted corpse was placed where ships passing in and out of a harbor or estuary could see it," Vallar explained. "They served as warnings to all sailors that those who deigned to follow in the pirates' footsteps would meet a similar gruesome fate. Problem was that in the grand scheme of things, most sailors who went on the account either died from other causes or were never caught and punished."

Peter Muise, author of *Legends and Lore of the North Shore*, told me that Nix's Mate was much larger four hundred years ago. "Records indicate the island had an area of twelve acres when it was deeded to one John Gallop in 1636 for sheep grazing. It currently has an area of about zero acres," Muise said.

What happened to all the land, and how did the island get its bizarre name?

"According to legend, in the 1630s, a first mate on a ship moored off the island was accused of murdering his captain while he slept," said Muise. "The captain's last name was Nix. After a hasty trial, the mate was found guilty and sentenced to be hanged on the island. Nix's mate protested that he was innocent, but his pleas fell on deaf ears."

The man allegedly cursed the island, begging God to prove he was accused of a crime he didn't commit. "Show that I am innocent," Nix's mate supposedly uttered. "Let this island sink into the sea to prove that I have never committed murder." Nix's mate was executed. Soon after, the island did start to sink into the harbor. However, erosion seems to be the cause—not some curse uttered by a soon-to-be-executed deckhand.

Muise said that a second, more fantastic variant of the Nix's Mate legend exists. It involves a role reversal. "Captain Nix was a pirate who got rich raiding merchant vessels," he recalled. "One night he rowed to the island with a chest full of gold and his loyal first mate. After the mate dug a pit, the captain killed him and buried him with the gold. His restless spirit guards the treasure but also apparently caused the island to sink into the sea."

For the record, no reports exist of a man bearing his name. Nor are there any accounts of a pirate known as Captain Nix committing murder or being killed.

The third theory behind Nix's Mate's name involves the Dutch phrase "nixie shmalt," which refers to the haunting cry of water spirits. According to legend, a sailor from the Netherlands uttered the phrase while listening to the ghostly waves wallop the island's shore.

Muise said we'll probably never know for sure how Nix's Mate got its name. He also said the "sinking curse" is more based on legend than fact. "Historians claim it has shrunk over time simply because it was quarried for shale and ship's ballast in the 1700s," Muise explained. "After these large stones were removed, the tides eroded the rest of the island. That explanation makes sense, but somehow the stories about pirates and ghosts seem more fitting for this tiny but mysterious island."

Boston Harbor ferries and passengers who regularly sail by Nix's Mate en route to Georges Island in the outer harbor say a weird energy surrounds the tiny island. The *Provincetown III* got stuck in its rocky shoals on August 25, 2012, while heading from Boston to Provincetown. No injuries were reported, but it's common for captains to lose radio connection near Nix's Mate.

There are also more sinister reports. Locals believe that William Fly continues to linger on the rocky shoals as a harbinger of injustice. "On the island that is slowly succumbing to the ocean, sailors have reported seeing mysterious lights, hearing bloodcurdling screams and uneasy laughs, as well as awkward whispers," claimed Christopher Forest in *Boston's Haunted History*. "Many speculate that the spirit of the violent pirate roams the island patrolling the land and calling to all sailors as they pass by."

Truthfully, Fly's ghost doesn't have much room to roam around Nix's Mate. It's almost completely submerged during high tide, except for a few rocks assembled in an odd pattern. Believe it or not, the configuration of the exposed rock looks like the perfect shape of a question mark, further punctuating Boston Harbor's freak of nature.

Crime Q&A:
Thomas D'Agostino

*Legends are a romantic part of our past despite the fact
that they're sometimes embellished out of proportion by
fertile imaginations.*

—Thomas D'Agostino

Thomas D'Agostino, author of several paranormal-themed books including *Legends, Lore and Secrets of New England*, is the go-to expert when one is looking for weird stories of murder and mayhem from the Bay State's bloodstained past. In fact,

PHOTO COURTESY THOMAS D'AGOSTINO

he has an encyclopedic mind full of strange tales from the crypt including an "ordeal of touch" case in seventeenth-century Boston involving cruentation.

"A woman was convicted and executed based on this belief," D'Agostino told me. The pre-forensics technique involved bringing in the alleged assailant who then had to interact with the victim postmortem. "If the actual murderer were to touch the victim's corpse, the body would then begin to bleed where it was touched," he explained. "It was an odd but frequently used way of detecting a killer."

Of course, this medieval approach to a murder investigation is extremely flawed. However, it didn't stop the Puritans. Mary Martin, a woman from the Massachusetts Bay Colony, was hanged on March 18, 1647, after the "ordeal of touch" was administered on her stillborn infant. After the courtroom test, which involved the woman touching the dead face of her child, Martin broke down in tears and confessed.

In the interview, D'Agostino talked about several crime-related legends pulled from the books he coauthors with his partner, Arlene Nicholson. Ever hear of the murder-solving parrot in Halifax, Massachusetts? D'Agostino confirmed that the talon-toed Perry Mason somehow cracked the case. Nope. It's definitely not one for the birds.

Q: Why do you think New England's legends and lore are so weird?

A: There are many cultures and societies that have settled here. Each brought their own beliefs and superstitions. What might be strange to one is a normal custom to another. Over time, some of these were mixed together, creating an even stranger system of ideals that are the stuff legends are made from.

Q: Speaking of weird legends, what's the strangest story involving a supposed murder in Massachusetts that you've uncovered?
A: I have to say the story where the parrot solved a triple murder in Halifax, Massachusetts, in the nineteenth century. When the suspect was taken to the murder scene, the parrot began crying out, 'Murderer, murderer,' when he passed by the bird.

Q: Have you noticed any recurring themes in the ghost lore that you've written about?
A: There are many, but for the most part, victims of an untimely death, abandoned villages where spirits once traversed in mortal form, vampires, witches, and revenge seem to be the most popular recurring themes in New England.

Q: What do these scary stories say about us and our puritanical past?
A: The early fears of witches and the devil may have played a part in older legends, but with the Great Awakening, the puritanical thought became obsolete. Yet, the tales still remained, and new ones joined them in the pages of our arcane history. Also, there are many Native American ghost stories that don't fall into any realm of puritan belief but still took root.

Q: Do you think crime scenes are more prone to hauntings than other locations?

A: Not necessarily. I believe that if the area has energy residing to begin with, then a violent act may take root and remain for centuries. It's a scarring of the earth, but that doesn't mean every crime scene can become haunted. I feel there must be that energy pocket ready to capture it like a camera or video captures the moment.

Q: Any details on the "Witch Rock Murders" in Rochester, Massachusetts?

A: According to the legend, a woman fled persecution in Salem during the witch hysteria and was captured at the rock. Her captors murdered her for being a witch right then and there. This may have helped fuel the legend of the rock where it was once told that witches could be seen flying out of the rock.

Q: What are your thoughts regarding the accuracy of legends in New England? Should we debunk them if it's not based on historical fact?

A: All legends are based on some fact, even if there's just a thread of truth. Because of my historical background and the desire to know the whole truth behind every story I have ever written or read about, I've debunked many legends including my all-time favorites only to be disappointed with the actual truth versus the accepted legend. Legends are a romantic part of our past despite the fact that they're sometimes embellished out of proportion by fertile imaginations.

Q: Anything else?

A: New England is one of the richest if not the number one place in the world for unbelievable legends, folklore, and haunts. It's an honor to live here and be able to write about and share all the incredible stories that have emerged from this region.

The Legends

Watch out for the Black Widow!
—The Gloucester Telegraph, January 1862

One of Boston's most notorious hauntings centers on the ghost of a Confederate prisoner's wife who was allegedly sentenced to death for aiding in the escape of a soldier when Georges Island's historic Fort Warren served as a Civil War lockup. She's known as the Lady in Black.

Georges Island's
Lady in Black

The Lady in Black summoned me here. However, as I searched every nook and cranny of Georges Island during a five-month gig as a historical narrator in Boston Harbor, the ghost of Melanie Lanier—as the Lady in Black is otherwise called—refused to reveal herself. She was playing hard to get.

"Something touched me in there, and it wasn't human," screamed a girl running out of the corridor of dungeons after a field trip to Fort Warren at Georges Island. "It was the Lady in Black," she said convincingly.

The girl looked mortified.

This was just one of the strange events that occurred during the summer of 2014, when I gave historical tours with Boston Harbor Cruises and traveled on large vessels carrying passengers back and forth to various islands in the outer harbor. I spent most afternoons during the summer searching for a repeat experience of a shadow figure, which I'd seen there seven years before. No luck.

I frequently heard screams emanating from Fort Warren's haunted ramparts. However, it was usually one of the kids touring the dark hallway in the southeast battery.

For the record, the location that Edward Rowe Snow said was the Lady in Black's haunt was in the front of the fort. It's still accessible but extremely dusty and dark.

In 2007, I moved back to Boston from Florida and had a ghostly experience while touring the ramparts of Fort Warren at Georges Island. Out of the corner of my eye, I noticed an all-black shadow figure. I looked again, and it was gone. At this point, I had never heard of the Lady in Black legend. I just intuitively knew Georges Island had some sort of psychic residue. While researching Fort Warren's history, my interest in Boston's haunted past gradually became a passion. History repeats itself, and it was my job to uncover the truth and give a voice to those without a voice—even though most of the stories turned out to be tales from the crypt.

Lawrence, a fellow Boston Harbor Cruises tour guide and former park ranger, insisted that ghosts do not inhabit Georges Island, adding that the Lady in Black legend was completely made up by folklorist Edward Rowe Snow.

"I spent so many nights there, I would know," he said as we passed Nix's Mate en route to the mainland. "However, I would say the island has a spirit. Some rangers say the island's energy, or spirit, welcomes people."

In hindsight, I've decided that my encounter on Georges in 2007 was the island's spirit welcoming me. However, ghosts can almost certainly be found nearby.

While several of the thirty-four islands have paranormal activity, Boston Harbor's Little Brewster is allegedly the most haunted. The mysterious Boston Light, one of the five remaining Coast Guard–manned lighthouses in America, stands eerily on the rocky, two-acre island. It's located behind Georges Island and can be spotted from the ramparts, which I explored regularly during the summer of 2014. While I was giving historical tours, the lighthouse was closed for much-needed repairs in preparation for its 300-year anniversary.

Boston Light reopened in 2015 and has once again become a Boston Harbor hot spot.

Photographer Frank C. Grace, his father, and I took a ferry out to Little Brewster. It was a rainy, overcast day . . . perfect weather for a ghostly encounter. Coincidentally, we visited hours before Boston Light's anniversary, and the island was buzzing with excitement from both the living and the dead. The volunteers at the historic lighthouse were quick to confirm that Little Brewster was indeed haunted.

"You hear ghost stories all the time," remarked Val, a veteran tour guide. "One day, I had climbed all the way to the top, and I heard phantom footsteps behind me, and there was definitely no one else in the lighthouse."

Other volunteers have mentioned hearing what sounds like congo drums, possibly Native American tribal rhythms, on the island—without a plausible explanation.

Jeremy D'Entremont, historian for the American Lighthouse Foundation and author of *The Lighthouse Handbook New England,* confirmed the ghostly legends associated with Boston Light. "Coast Guard keepers experienced odd things and generally blamed it on 'George,' meaning George Worthylake, the first keeper, who drowned in 1718," he told me. "The Coast Guard

Auxiliary Watchstanders, who spend shifts there today, have also seen strange things."

On the way back, we passed many of the islands I fell in love with during the summer of 2014. Nix's Mate, the smallest of the Harbor Islands, seemed particularly ominous. Marked by a black-and-white beacon and completely submerged during high tide, the freakishly small island is where pirates were kept in a crude contraption known as a gibbet cage, an invention of the Puritans. They would showcase the pirates as sort of a cautionary tale. While narrating Boston Harbor tours, I was pushed from my seat by an unseen force multiple times when passing this spot. It was so intense that I physically tied myself to my chair. One time I was pushed so hard that I almost fell off the top deck of the vessel.

Disgruntled ghost pirates? Yep, Boston Harbor has them.

While giving tours during the summer of 2014, a coworker at Boston Harbor Cruises captured an electronic voice phenomenon while exploring Georges Island one afternoon. He spent the day with his brother exploring the fort and captured a voice of what sounded like a man. "You can hear breathing and then it says some-thing," he told me, playing the recording over and over.

"It sounds like it says 'get out' or something similar," I told him.

What's even more fascinating is that the male voice saying "get out" in his impromptu EVP sounded Southern. Could it be a Confederate soldier?

One year later, I ventured out to Fort Warren and crawled through the original corridor of dungeons. I found the coffin used by Edward Rowe Snow to retell the Lady in Black legend. It was covered in dust and cobwebs.

A message from the vice president of the Confederacy, Alexander Hamilton Stephens, popped into my head. His quote: "All the genius I have lies in this."

I laughed. It all made sense now. There is no Lady in Black. The ghost is a Confederate soldier or possibly even the cranky spirit of Stephens. I shivered in the beauty and the madness of the moment.

I crawled out of Fort Warren's corridor of dungeons armed with my latest tale from the crypt. Melanie Lanier is totally made up. The Lady in Black is a man.

LADY IN BLACK'S HAUNT: FORT WARREN

BOSTON HARBOR, MA—One of Boston's most notorious hauntings centers on the ghost of a Confederate prisoner's wife who was sentenced to death for aiding in the escape of a soldier when Georges Island's historic Fort Warren served as a Civil War lockup.

According to the legend popularized by historian Edward Rowe Snow, a gun-toting Southern woman named Melanie Lanier disguised herself as a male prisoner, snuck into the fort in an attempt to free her newlywed husband, and managed to infiltrate his cell. When the duo were approached by Fort Warren's Colonel Justin Dimick, the wife haphazardly fired her pistol and killed her husband instead. When the gutsy woman from North Carolina was sent to the gallows, her last request was to wear female clothing, which came in the form of a makeshift black robe whipped together by Union soldiers. She's known as the Lady in Black.

Located seven miles offshore from downtown Boston, Georges Island is one of the more popular stops on the Boston Harbor Islands ferry tour and was used as farmland before it was acquired by the government for coastal defense. Built in 1847, the island's Fort Warren is a ghostly, pentagonal-shaped granite structure once used as a training camp, a sentry post, and a prison for Confederate soldiers during the Civil War. It also defended Boston during the Spanish-American War and through World Wars I and II before it was decommissioned in 1947.

The first Confederate war prisoners arrived at Fort Warren on October 31, 1861. Colonel Dimick, a West Point graduate and Mexican War veteran, anticipated housing 150 prisoners. According to newspaper reports in 1861, more than 800 Confederate soldiers arrived at the ill-prepared Fort Warren, and a feeling of "pity rather than . . . hatred of the visitors" was exacerbated by the distressed state of the fort. Despite the less-than-stellar conditions, Dimick was lauded for his humane treatment of the prisoners, while Bostonians rallied to help with food rations and bedding, hoping that the Union war prisoners would receive equally hospitable care.

However, the so-called Lady in Black didn't fare so well. According to Snow's story, reprinted in Jay Schmidt's book *Fort Warren*, "Colonel Dimick had no alternative but to sentence her to hang as a spy." Snow's legend recounted several sightings of the black widow apparition. Three nineteenth-century soldiers noticed mysterious footprints in the shape of a woman's shoes in the snow.

In 1934, a sergeant reportedly heard a female voice warning him, saying, "Don't come in here!" when he approached the fort's dungeon area. Soldiers on sentry duty shot at ghostlike apparitions and claimed they'd been chased by the lady of the black robes. Guards stationed at the fort during World War II would taunt new recruits when it was time for duty, telling the newbies to "watch out for the Black Widow!" The *Gloucester Telegraph*, in January 1862, reported that soldiers spotted a supernatural presence of an old woman who was "vindictively frisking about the ruins of an old building from which she was ejected some time previous to her death."

Gerard Butler, a former curator at Fort Warren during the 1970s, told Schmidt in an interview that he had a few paranormal encounters while living on Georges Island. "He heard the distinctive clicking sounds of footsteps coming toward him along the ramparts," Schmidt wrote in *Fort Warren*, adding that Butler's wife and daughter were both asleep during the alleged incident. Butler also said that a police dog stationed at the fort in the late 1960s was afraid of the structure's Bastion A area. "The dog would go anywhere in the fort, but once it got to Bastion A, the dog would always refuse to go inside," Butler recounted. In 1981, a crew of Civil War reenactors saw a dark shadowy figure creeping in the night and watched in awe as a lantern levitated through the ramparts without a living person holding it.

To add to the Lady in Black mystery, no recorded accounts have been found of a woman being hanged as a spy. In fact, similarly, no reports of Confederate soldiers or sympathizers being executed at Fort Warren during the Civil War have come to light.

Union soldier deaths? Yep. There were two documented executions on April 22, 1864—those of Matthew Riley and Charles Carpenter, who had notoriously joined a military unit, collected the bonus, and then deserted. They were marched to the right side of the fort's demilune and were fatally shot by a squad of riflemen. Today, the execution site is a picnic area. There may have been more executions on Georges Island, but the paperwork documenting Fort Warren's haunted past was destroyed when the military compound was decommissioned after World War II.

However, Butler said a crew of Massachusetts Institute of Technology (MIT) students may have conjured up the lady of the black robes in the mid-1970s. He recalled seeing a photograph shot by MIT students who set up a camera at Fort Warren's Scarp Gallery to record paranormal activity. The former curator said that one photo strangely resembled the so-called Lady in Black. "It did look as if there was a woman apparition facing the camera with a sun bonnet and shawl," he said, adding that "it could have been air currents or a fog or something." Butler even mused that the photo may have been one of MIT's infamous hacks or "a mild hoax for intra-office chuckles" at the university.

Or it could have been the residual spirit of the Lady in Black taking her nightly stroll along the fort's ramparts in search of the man she murdered by mistake.

CRIME PROFILE: PETER MUISE

People see a ghostly figure in black and need to explain
why this figure appears on Georges Island. Voila!
The legend of the Lady in Black is born.
—Peter Muise, *New England Folklore*

Peter Muise, author of *Legends and Lore of the North Shore* and
founder of the blog *New England Folklore*, said there's something
mysterious and oddly fascinating about Boston Harbor's series
of forts. Many of these historic structures, he noted, are in an
arrested state of decay, which only adds to their spooky mystique.

"Boston has a long history and for many years was one of
North America's most important port cities. The forts were built
to defend the city from attacks by sea," he explained. "The first
forts were built by the English to protect the city from enemies
like the French but also probably from random pirate attacks.
When the American Revolution started, the British used the
forts to control access to the harbor and as shelter from the

PHOTO COURTESY PETER MUISE

Americans. After the Revolution, the Americans used the forts to defend the city from the British in the War of 1812, and during the Civil War, the forts helped protect Boston from attacks by the Confederacy. Some of the harbor forts were also fitted with anti-aircraft guns during World War II."

As New England's legends-and-lore expert, Muise said the forts dotting the islands of Boston Harbor are rich with stories, adding that a lot of ghosts believed to be haunting the waters of Boston Harbor got their origins from real-life horrors. "Many traumatic events have happened on the islands," Muise continued. "Executions, massacres, shipwrecks, war, and deaths from disease. Some people believe that traumas like those cause ghosts and other paranormal activities."

One of those ghost stories—the legend of the Lady in Black—has taken on a life of its own thanks to the work of author and folklorist Edward Rowe Snow. "Well, the Lady in Black is the best-known ghost on the harbor islands, and local folklorist Edward Rowe Snow helped spread her legend after Fort Warren opened to the public in 1961," continued Muise. "However, there's no historic record that a woman was ever hanged at Fort Warren, so a lot of people assume that Snow created the story himself."

While the legend of Melanie Lanier—who apparently dressed as a man to save her Confederate soldier husband but ended up accidentally killing him—may be completely fabricated, Muise said there's some truth behind the elaborate backstory. "Snow didn't completely make up the legend of the Lady in Black," said Muise. "Historian Jay Schmidt notes that soldiers stationed at the fort during World War II did tell stories about a ghostly black widow who haunted the island and also mentions other ghost stories he was told himself, like a ghostly lantern that has been seen floating through the air, carried by unseen hands."

It's clear from these reports that the Lady in Black phenomenon is partly based on face-to-face encounters with the paranormal. However, the story, which centers on a Southern woman who was rumored to be hanged on Georges Island, is a form of poetic license, used to explain the unexplainable. "I don't think her story is necessarily based on a real woman, but I don't think it is entirely fabricated either," he added. "It's probably based on real experiences that people have had. People see a ghostly figure in black and need to explain why this figure appears on Georges Island. Voila! The legend of the Lady in Black is born."

While the Lady in Black myth and other Boston Harbor ghost lore intrigue Muise, he's equally fascinated with the bizarre real-life stories that have emerged from Boston Harbor's forts. One story involved the larger-than-life rats found on Lovells and Georges Island.

"Back during the Civil War, there used to be a lot of rats on the island," Muise said. "They lived off the food refuse from the mess hall and dug their warrens deep under the stone walls. They were quite a nuisance, but the troops had other concerns, so the rats just kept multiplying. One day, one of the soldiers stationed on the island went into Boston to get a haircut. He kept his hair long—as was the fashion then—and had the barber style it with a pomade made from lard and sweet fragrances."

Muise said the soldier returned to Georges Island with a stylish new haircut. However, the man was plagued with dreams of buzzing mosquitoes while trying to sleep in his makeshift Fort Warren bed. "When he woke up, he was shocked to find that all his hair was gone," Muise explained with a laugh. "The rats in the walls had been attracted to the sweet lard smell of pomade, and they had devoured his hair while he slept."

Muise continued: "Their gnawing had filtered into his dreams as the sound of mosquitoes. To add insult to injury, his hair never grew back."

Hoosac Tunnel's Bloody Pit

Is the Hoosac Tunnel in North Adams, Massachusetts, cursed? Based purely on the tunnel's bloody backstory, it's definitely possible.

Michael Norman and Beth Scott wrote about the haunted history associated with the so-called bloody pit in *Historic Haunted America*. "The digging of this railroad tunnel is a saga of blood, sweat, and tears. Begun in 1851, it wasn't finished until 1875. During those twenty-four years, hundreds of miners, using mostly crude black powder and pick and shovel, chipped away at the unyielding rock of Hoosac Mountain," Norman and Scott wrote. "By the time the tunnel was finished, 200 men had lost their lives in what came to be known as 'the bloody pit.' Most died in explosions, fires, and drownings, but one death may not have been accidental."

Peter Muise, author of *Legends and Lore of the North Shore*, told me that there were unexpected hurdles from the get-go. "People in North Adams decided to dig a tunnel through the mountain because there was no other way around it," he said. "They built this giant drilling machine, and it immediately broke down and got stuck in the rock."

And then there was the case of two accidental deaths that may have resulted in a revenge killing. "If you're looking for murders, there's Ringo Kelley," Muise said. "He had a great name. Unfortunately, he met a very bad end."

Two men, Ned Brinkman and Billy Nash, were killed during a nitroglycerin-induced explosion on March 20, 1865. Kelley, the man who prematurely set off the explosion, managed to escape the wrath of the bloody pit that afternoon, but one year later he mysteriously disappeared. Kelley's body was found two miles inside of the Hoosac Tunnel, at the exact spot where Brinkman and Nash had died. He'd been strangled to death. There were no suspects . . . at least among the living.

How did Kelley die? Ghost lore enthusiasts claimed that Kelley was murdered by the vengeful spirits of Brinkman and Nash. Muise told me that the evidence found at the scene doesn't add up to a postmortem revenge killing. "It couldn't have been the ghosts of the two victims because they found the rope around Kelley's neck," he told me. "Where had he been the year prior? Who strangled him? These things have never been resolved."

Over the years, multiple sources who were brave enough to venture inside the Hoosac Tunnel claimed to see phantom miners and hear mysterious groans. One man, Frank Webster, said he was summoned inside the bloody pit in 1874 by a voice in the darkness. Webster then said he saw floating apparitions. One of the apparitions supposedly grabbed Webster's rifle and hit him over the head with it. He was missing for three days and later told authorities about his close encounter in the tunnel. According to the police report, when Webster showed up, his rifle was missing, and he looked like he'd seen a ghost.

"Given its history, there are a lot of weird legends associated with the Hoosac Tunnel," Muise explained. "Even after the tunnel was done, bad things happened. People who worked on the trains that went through the tunnel claimed that they had seen headless ghosts. They would also see phantom shapes carrying lights in there."

Muise said there are reports of people mysteriously disappearing in the bloody pit. "One man from North Adams decided to walk through the tunnel. People saw him walk in, and he was going to come out the other end in Florida, Massachusetts," Muise said. "He never came out. No one ever found him."

As far as his personal experiences exploring the Hoosac Tunnel, Muise said he never actually made it inside the bloody pit. "It's definitely a creepy place," he said. "There was this cold, dank air, and I was like, 'I'm not stepping foot in that tunnel.' It's built on an incline to let water drain out, but it means you can't see through it. So, if you're standing on one end, you can't see the light from the other end."

Muise's words of wisdom? "If you do go inside, you're going to be in complete darkness for two and a half miles. It's unnerving, plus trains still go through the tunnel. My advice? Don't go inside."

BLOODY PIT'S HAUNT: HOUGHTON MANSION

NORTH ADAMS, MA—Sensitives to the paranormal claimed to be stricken with sadness as soon as they entered the Houghton Mansion in North Adams back when the haunted hot spot hosted public ghost hunts. Purchased by a private developer in October 2017, the structure's new owners have closed their doors to investigations.

However, it doesn't mean that the Houghton Mansion isn't paranormally active. In fact, the investigators and researchers that I've talked to over the years believe the North Adams property has a legacy of being the state's most haunted.

Based on my brief but memorable visit to the property in 2015, it was a bit overwhelming walking into the majestic old house built by Albert C. Houghton, a millionaire and North Adams's first mayor. It's almost as if the guilt associated with a tragedy in 1914 has psychically imprinted itself onto the walls of the former Masonic Temple located at 172 Church Street.

So, what happened more than a century ago to the Houghton family?

It all started with a casual drive at 9:00 a.m. on August 1, 1914. What happened next caused a ripple effect that destroyed the family and left an indelible mark on the mansion. Houghton asked his employee, John Widders, to rev up their new Pierce-Arrow touring car and drive his family and friends along the winding roads that cut through the picturesque mountains of North Adams. Houghton's wife, Cordelia, decided to stay home that fateful day.

While they were en route to Bennington, Vermont, Widders hit a soft shoulder on the road after swerving around a team of horses. The car then tumbled down an embankment and flipped three times. The men, including Houghton and Widders, escaped with minor injuries.

The patriarch's daughter, Mary, died in the North Adams hospital immediately after the impact and so did her childhood friend, Sybil Hutton. Widders, overwhelmed with grief, lifted a horse pistol to his temple and committed suicide in the cellar of the mansion's barn. Houghton, who was expected to survive the accident, returned to his home and died ten days later. His injuries from the car crash were fatal, but many believe he actually died from heartbreak after losing his beloved daughter so tragically.

Paranormal investigators claimed that an aura of destruction has psychically imprinted itself on the Houghton Mansion.

I visited the location in early August, a few days after the 101-year anniversary of the Houghton tragedy, and was immediately overwhelmed with sadness. Joni Mayhan, author of *Bones in the Basement* and featured investigator of the evening, said it was common for sensitives to pick up on the energy still lingering in the home. My documentary crew interviewed the author minutes before her overnight investigation.

"It's very active," Mayhan told me. "The last time I was here, I actually saw an apparition in the basement. It was the bottom of a little girl's dress. In the past, we've caught a lot of EVPs here."

After we left, she said all hell broke loose during what was her fifth visit to the North Adams hot spot.

"I was well-versed on the history and had a good idea what to expect," Mayhan explained on her blog. "While I was excited to be returning to one of my favorite haunts, I was looking forward to the social aspect more than the actual haunting. I would be in for a shock. My fifth visit was a wild ride I will never forget."

Mayhan told me that before the investigation, she wasn't convinced the mansion was one of the Bay State's most haunted locations. However, her tune quickly changed. After the investigation, she was convinced that something much darker had made a home for itself in the bowels of the Houghton Mansion.

"I knew there was a dark entity in the basement of the mansion. We encountered him there several times before and saw him in the form of dark shadows moving in the darkness," Mayhan explained. "There was also supposed to be a little girl there who answers to the name Laura. While the Houghtons had a daughter named Laura who died at the age of three, many aren't convinced this is the same little girl. They theorize that the mansion was built on an existing foundation, so the ghost of the child could belong to the first house that sat on the property."

Mayhan said she saw a dark shadow pacing back and forth in front of a doorway in the basement.

"As we settled into the session, the mediums in the group could feel an energy building. The darkness grew to epic proportions, filling the room with a sense of anger and loathing that even the non-mediums could feel," Mayhan recalled. "At one point, one member of the group became so overwhelmed with the dark energy, she needed to remove herself from the building to recoup her energy."

Mayhan picked up an EVP that could be labeled as Class A. The disembodied voice said: "Sit down." Based on the tone of the recording, the energy sounded aggressive.

The insults continued in Mary Houghton's bedroom. The EVPs Mayhan captured were overtly antagonistic. A male voice insulted one of the women in the room and called another investigator a "fat bastard." After a psychic identified an older female spirit hiding in the corner and asked who was standing before her, the male voice spoke through the spirit box, saying "it's that poor bitch."

On the third floor, there's a locker room that was used by the Masons after they purchased the mansion in the 1920s. The women felt uncomfortable on the third floor, and when Mayhan asked if they should leave the locker room, an EVP responded: "If you could."

The crew from the Travel Channel's *Ghost Adventures* had an equally memorable "lockdown" when they investigated the Houghton Mansion in 2008.

"Nestled in the heart of the Berkshire Mountains is one of New England's most mysterious and haunted buildings," said Zak Bagans. "Before we get locked down, I want to learn about the history. There's a lot of dark history about this place, and I hear there are some tragic events that happened to the family that built this place, the Houghton family. They're the ones said to haunt this place." Bagans added that the mansion was home to a Masonic temple but its "dark history began in the early 1900s."

The masons who frequented the location confirmed the hauntings to Bagans. "Nearly every time I come down, you hear a door slam or footsteps," said Nick Montello. Mason Randy Ransford said doors mysteriously open and close when no one else is there.

One of the masons told Bagans that the property is lined with granite boulders taken from the Hoosac Tunnel, also known as the "bloody pit." Bagans intimated that the Houghton tragedy could have been somehow tied to those rocks.

Mayhan told me that Bagans's "Hoosac Tunnel curse" theory is definitely viable. "Yes, it's possible that all of the negative energy, all of the death and destruction in the Hoosac Tunnel, was somehow absorbed and then transferred here."

Bagans's theory—that the granite boulders taken from the Hoosac Tunnel and placed on the Houghtons' property somehow cursed the land—is compelling. The actual *Ghost Adventures* investigation uncovered some convincing evidence including an inexplicable mist in Mary Houghton's room. For the record, previous investigators have captured EVPs of ghostly screams and a menacing voice from beyond that commanded the investigators to "get out."

There are also photos of a ghostly face peeking out of the third-floor window. Not surprisingly, it's on the top floor where the servants, including Houghton's chauffeur, Widders, once lived. Neighbors also said they've seen lights on in the third floor, which is impossible as there's no electricity on the top level.

Like Mayhan, Bagans encountered something paranormal in the basement of the Houghton Mansion. He captured a voice of an older man clearly saying, "Ran for help." Was it Widders, Houghton's driver, professing his guilty conscience in the afterlife? It's hard to tell. There are so many layers to the multiple spirits inhabiting this extremely haunted hot spot in North Adams.

Salem's Blue Lady

When it comes to the hocus pocus related to some of the dramatic ghost lore associated with Salem, Massachusetts, there's one boo-tiful lady who has become the belle of Essex Street.

The story of Salem's Lady in the Blue Dress or Blue Lady has gotten more elaborate over the years, with some claiming that the alleged murder victim was pregnant and was meeting her suitor with the hopes that they would get married. According to the ever-changing legend, she was attacked as she was waiting for her beloved. While the perpetrator is different based on each retelling, I've also heard from various guides that her sailor boyfriend was the one who actually murdered her.

When I first started giving tours in Salem, I was told that the Lady in Blue was breaking up a fight with her boyfriend and another sailor. As she was trying to stop the quarrel, the young woman was accidentally killed. My take on the so-called tragedy is the man was alone with her and snapped when he heard that she was pregnant with his baby. He then fatally bludgeoned the poor lady who supposedly wore a blue dress.

How the woman was murdered has been told differently over the years. Some tour guides believe she was hit over the head with a rock or slammed against a brick wall. Others claimed that she was stabbed. However, the accepted version of the tale was that a woman was left for dead in the tunnel after she was accidentally shot. The men who killed her confessed their sin to the reverend of the First Church, who, years later, burdened with the guilt of the knowledge of the murder, hanged himself in the top floor of the church, leaving a note detailing the crime. According to locals, the reverend is often seen haunting the second floor of the historic Daniel Low building—typically through the windows that face Essex Street.

In an episode of *Most Terrifying Places* that aired on the Travel Channel, I recounted the heartbreaking legend of the Lady in the Blue Dress on camera, recorded in the dusty bowels of the haunted brick building that is now home to Rockafellas. The land located on the corner of Washington and Essex Streets was where Salem's first meetinghouse was located from 1634 to 1673. For the record, the spot where the actual Salem Witch Trials took place was farther down Washington Street, located in present-day Salem Cycles.

While I'm not convinced the Blue Lady's backstory is actually true, I do think her story has been told so often that we've actually created a "thought form" or *tulpa*, the mystical concept that a being or an object can be created through spiritual or mental powers.

When I recounted my face-to-face encounter with a shadow figure on the Travel Channel's *Most Terrifying Places*, I also discussed a possible tie to the Blue Lady based on a creepy experience that I had while working the overnight shift at the Hotel Salem on Essex Street. The boutique hotel is only a few blocks away from the Daniel Low building, and I regularly passed by Rockafellas when I headed into work. When I accepted the night auditor position at the Hotel Salem, I asked the manager if there were any reports of hauntings, and he said, "No, because it scares away business," but that didn't stop my ongoing experiences working the paranormal nightshift, specifically when I spent time in the lower-level area.

The hotel's under-construction kitchen located in the basement creeped me out the most. The lights flickered regularly, and one time the bulbs went out and started to illuminate almost like a runway as if something was passing by each light and causing it to turn on and off. I also heard what sounded like phantom footsteps, and, in one horrifying incident, I saw what looked like a man's footprint emerge in sawdust residue left on the floor.

However, nothing prepared me for what was arguably the scariest night of my life. It was around 3:00 a.m. in early January 2018, and I was making coffee for the hotel's guests in the lower level of the repurposed brick building that once served as a department store known as Newmark's. I heard what sounded like someone taking a piece of metal and a hammer and banging it loudly next door. The lights in the basement started to flicker again, and then I heard what sounded like a man in pain. He was moaning and not in a good way.

I ran upstairs, thinking it was someone outside. Because I'm friends with the owners of Wicked Good Books, I looked in the window of the bookstore on Essex Street to make sure no one was trying to break into the store or the neighboring Magic Parlor.

What I saw that night has haunted me for years. While I was peeking through the windows, I saw what looked like a shadow figure dart by the window of Wicked Good Books. The entity seemed to be wearing a hat. I thought that it was one of the employees, perhaps, working a late-night shift. I looked again, and the "hat man" was gone. In the heat of the moment, I assumed that the shadow figure was something that could be explained, and I was hoping that it was merely a reflection from the street lights.

Then I heard a bloodcurdling scream, and my internal alarms kicked into high gear. It sounded like a woman crying for help, and it was coming from the dark alley next to Rockafellas. I ran over to the Daniel Low building, expecting to encounter someone being attacked. There was no one there.

The following day, I asked the manager of the Essex Street shop if anybody was working a late-night shift at Wicked Good Books. Nope. Replaying the episode from the previous night and not finding a logical explanation, I was terrified. I ended up leaving my job at the hotel a few days after that incident because I was too creeped out to continue.

In hindsight, I believe the "hat man" was trying to tell me something. But what about the mysterious scream coming from the alley behind Rockafellas? During the recording of *Most Terrifying Places*, I suggested that it's somehow tied to the Lady in the Blue Dress legend. Could it be a residual haunting or videotaped replay of a traumatic event? Yes, it's possible.

BLUE LADY'S HAUNT: ROCKAFELLAS

SALEM, MA—Truthfully, you can't walk a block in the Witch City without passing a building with a haunted reputation. However, the ghosts supposedly inhabiting Rockafellas on the corner of Washington and Essex Streets are among the city's more notorious, thanks to the lore associated with the legendary Blue Lady. In fact, the restaurant named a specialty cocktail after her called the Lady in the Blue Dress, made with rum and blue curacao. According to the menu, "After this one, you may see her."

Who is this Blue Lady spirit? "She's supposedly the specter of an employee who died where Rockafellas now stands, back when the site was Daniel Low & Co., a pioneering department store," wrote *Zagat* reporter Scott Kearnan. "The building also functioned as a church, which may explain sightings of a black-suited minister, and had plenty of other uses that add to its creepy character."

According to lore, the ghostly minister committed suicide when the building was a meetinghouse. He's been spotted in the downstairs area and is said to be a recluse. One report claimed the spirit said, "Git, I don't want to talk to you right now," when confronted.

The building's history is almost as interesting as the ghosts that allegedly linger there. Carved into the stone of a commemorative marker outside is the date 1932, which refers to Salem's First Church. The church used the building's second floor for worship and rented out the ground floor for various commercial establishments. Its past included a clothing shop for ladies and a dry goods store. Daniel Low moved into the structure in 1874, and his jewelry and gift business flourished. Low's bestseller? He created the souvenir witch spoon in the late 1800s, which launched Low's national mail-order business.

Low died from a heart-related illness in 1911. His son, Seth, continued the family legacy until 1939, when his widow took over. The historic building was eventually sold to William Follett in the 1950s. Rockafellas opened in 2003.

It's a little-known fact that the Daniel Low structure had a short stint as a live theater in 1828. "The building was actually erected four years earlier by a group of investors who wanted to bring live theater to Salem," reported the *Salem Evening News*. Its first production was called *Wives as They Were and Maids as They Were*. Apparently, Salem couldn't support the expenses associated with live performances. "Despite the excellent quality of this and subsequent productions, and the appearance of nationally known actors Edwin Forrest and Mary Duff, the Salem Theatre only lasted a few years."

The Blue Lady ghost made her debut appearance when Rockafellas opened. An employee shot a nighttime photo and posted it on the restaurant's website. In the picture is the full-bodied apparition of a lady who mysteriously appeared in front of the building. Rockafellas embraced its resident spirit and handed out T-shirts to patrons who claimed to have had a spirited encounter at the restaurant. The T-shirts read "Congratulations! You've Just Seen the Lady in the Blue Dress."

The lighthearted ghost lore turned dark when visitors, mainly women, claimed they spotted the lady in the downstairs hallway. Then there were screams. Several employees heard mysterious, disembodied cries—as if someone was buried alive—coming from the building's downstairs vault area. "Underground tunnels (now filled with concrete) once connected the site to other buildings around downtown Salem, and some of them were used as part of the Underground Railroad—leading to rumors that some slaves unsuccessfully seeking freedom were buried there," continued Kearnan. "The building was also a historic bank, and for the ultimate eerie factor, you can reserve a single table for two that sits in the former vault."

Ghost tours have elaborated over time with lore associated with the Blue Lady legend, suggesting that she was possibly murdered in the underground tunnels beneath the Daniel Low building. According to unsubstantiated lore, the woman was killed by her sailor boyfriend who buried her in the tunnels beneath the building. It's supposedly her eerie screams that echo in the lower-level vault area beneath Rockafellas.

True? Probably not. However, there's convincing evidence of desecrated human remains beneath the building. According to *Salem Secret Underground*, the building's underground system connected to an underground warehouse near the current Goddess Treasure Chest located in Derby Square. It's also where two runaway slaves are said to have been entombed. "The story goes that somewhere in Salem two gentlemen died and were not allowed a proper burial because their existence might hinder others who longed for freedom," wrote Christopher Dowgin. "So they encased them in a concrete tomb."

Yes, the underground network did exist. However, when William Follett bought the building in the 1950s, he had the underground tunnels filled in with concrete.

In honor of the mysterious cries from below, Rockafellas created a specialty drink called the Screaming Vault made with dark rums and juice. According to the menu, patrons can even keep the glass. Why? One of the many bizarre occurrences at the restaurant involves glass mysteriously breaking. Several visitors have watched in awe as their stemware shattered before their eyes. In another freaky encounter, a bartender claimed that a glass levitated from the bar's rack, bounced into the air, and landed on the counter without breaking. Now, that's a thirsty spirit.

S.K. Pierce Hauntings

Back in 2015, a woman named Mattie Cornwell summoned me to the haunted house in Gardner, Massachusetts. She's been dead for more than a century.

In the recurring dream, I saw her silhouette from a Victorian house's second floor. She's upset. I could see an outline of what looks like a tightly wound bun in her hair. Her clothing is late 1800s school marm, and she looks much older than her actual age. I would guess she's in her twenties. The woman is a caretaker of sorts and is protecting the home from forces out of her control. She's losing the battle and is calling me from the light for help.

Think Mary Poppins but without the spoonful of sugar. In my dream, she's serving up daggers.

Something horrible happened in that house, and she's begging the living to help her. I could hear her singing a folk song from the window. She was throwing books and papers at me from the home's second floor. She was saying what I remember as "sefnock" over and over at a shadowy man who is in the room with her. I'm terrified.

My dream of Mattie was in 2011. I was writing what would become my first book, *Ghosts of Boston*: *Haunts of the Hub*. I initially thought she was the "stay behind" spirit, the seamstress

I lovingly called "scissor sister," who haunted my home in Somerville's Davis Square.

I was wrong.

The dream was prophetic in a way. I didn't make a connection to the haunted S.K. Pierce Victorian Mansion in Gardner until I saw a photo of the structure posted online in late 2014. My friend Rachel Hoffman from Paranormal Xpeditions was investigating the location, and I had a severe reaction when I saw a post from the Victorian structure because I'd seen it repeatedly in my dreams.

I swore I would never go there. But I went anyway to the very spot where Mattie Cornwell once lived. What was I thinking?

A friend who has intuitive abilities warned me about the shadow figure in my dreams. "That woman will suck the air out of you," she said during an online chat. "No. I mean it. Like sitting on your chest. You won't be able to inhale." She said the spirit's name is Mattie or Matilda.

I found out recently from fellow author Joni Mayhan that the former nanny at the haunted S.K. Pierce Victorian was named Mattie Cornwell. Her spirit has been in the house since the late 1800s. "Petite, with long dark hair that she wore in a bun, she once cared for the Pierce children," wrote Mayhan in *Bones in the Basement*. "Chores were scheduled at specific times, and the children were taught to behave. Even though she was long dead, she remained the protector of the house, keeping it safe from trespassers and ensuring the other resident ghosts behaved themselves."

Mayhan said Cornwell had crossed over and was no longer bound to the haunted Victorian. "She was the Pierce family's nanny. Mattie wasn't negative, though. She was the gatekeeper and peacekeeper there, but she was inadvertently crossed over during a house cleansing in 2011," Mayhan told me. "After she left, the really nasty ones came in. There are a few nasty female entities there, but Mattie isn't one of them."

According to Mayhan's *Bones in the Basement*, Cornwell died young. "She was born in 1859 in Nova Scotia, Canada. She was 21 when she came to work for the Pierce family as a servant in the house. Her primary focus was caring for the Pierce children. She was firm but loving with the children, keeping them mindful of their manners and helping them grow into the influential men they would one day become," wrote Mayhan. "Later research would show that Mattie died at the young age of twenty-five from an acute inflammation of the hip just two years after getting married. Her tragedy would be just one among many at the Victorian mansion. It was as if the house collected them, like some people collect old coins."

Rachel Hoffman, my friend from the all-female investigation team Paranormal Xpeditions, said I should be wary about the haunted house in Gardner. "You might not be able to walk in," explained Hoffman. "I swear it's a pressure cooker. You will feel it as soon as you see it. Look into the top window and tell me what you see. Then I'll tell you."

Hoffman, who was featured in a taped investigation at the mansion with Tina Storer and her sister, Danielle Medina, said the experience still haunts her. She believes the location is a portal, a vortex of sorts, to the spirit world that allows both good and bad spirits to cross interdimensionally. "There's more than one story there," she said. "There's a story for every step you take."

When PXP was investigating the mansion in late 2014, I had a strong psychic feeling that one of the investigators, Storer, wasn't safe. I sent a message to the PXP team warning them. Hoffman told me later that Storer had to be escorted out of the building because she couldn't breathe. It was like the spirits were taking the air out of her lungs.

"Tina had issues where the man was burned," Hoffman told me. "At one point, she did feel protected. But it was so intense. Our temp gage was 66.6."

Medina, Hoffman's sister, was pregnant during the investigation, and the group uncovered an EVP in the nursery. "We got my pregnant sister bending over to pick up a baby in the nursery, and the ovilus said, 'Mama,'" explained Hoffman. "My sister is a skeptic, so this was profound."

Hoffman and the now-disbanded PXP team smudged the location with a cleansing ritual involving coffin nails and sweet grass. The usual sage simply didn't work. "When closing out a paranormal investigation, we sometimes use coffin nails," Hoffman explained. "I found our container used in the haunted Victorian Mansion with the bottom half of the glass jar totally gone. I wouldn't be surprised to find the nails we pounded in the ground embedded in a tree. Renovations and hands switching is stirring up the activity majorly."

Yes, construction notoriously conjures up the long departed. Apparently, spirits don't like change.

Rob Conti, the ringleader behind the New Jersey–based Dark Carnival and a dentist during the day, said he always wanted to own a haunted Victorian. The S.K. Pierce Mansion was literally ripped from his childhood fantasies. He said the fact that the 7,000-square-foot mansion located at 4 Broadway in Gardner is "certified haunted" was a bonus.

"Since I was fifteen, I always wanted a single-family haunted house," he said. "I always had a picture in my mind of what that would look like."

Conti, who actually didn't visit the Victorian until the day he closed the sale on the building in 2015, said a friend posted the real estate listing for the mansion on his Facebook page. "As soon as I saw it, I knew the image of the house was the image I had in my head for the past twenty-five years."

Since he and his wife, Allison, purchased what paranormal experts believe is the most haunted house in Massachusetts, Conti said he has been contacted by all sorts of people.

"I've been told that the spirits in the house knew who I was before I even called," he said, sort of creeped out by the idea. "Apparently, I'm liked by the spirits in the house, which is a good thing, I hope."

Conti also had a paranormal experience after walking into the structure's dining room, the same spot investigators believe was a portal. "I started feeling dizzy and had to be escorted out of the building," he explained. Also, the Dark Carnival owner said a contractor, who didn't know the building's haunted history, told him that somebody else was on the second floor when there was no one else in the house.

"I was also told by intuitives that the spirits in the house have something very important to tell me," Conti told me. "Does that sound crazy?"

Actually, no.

As I gazed at the house that haunted my dreams for years, I replayed the scene of the woman I believed to be Mattie Cornwell looking out of the second-floor window. As I walked closer to my nightmare, I start to hyperventilate. I think about the word "sefnock" that she chanted over and over. I hit my head as I quickly jumped into the car near the S.K. Pierce Mansion's driveway searching for a notepad. I wrote the mystery word out phonetically.

Then I had an epiphany. I gasped for air. The woman's cryptic, postmortem plea is backward. She's demanding that the shadow figure . . . confess.

Cars were driving by and passengers were yelling things at me like "There's someone behind you" and "This place is really, really haunted." My cell phone started to flip out and, mysteriously, seemed to have a mind of its own, calling random people from my contact list. I hear what sounds like a disembodied male voice whispering in my ear: "Get out of here."

I looked again at the second-floor window, expecting to see Mattie Cornwell, the spirit who mistakenly crossed to the light years ago. Instead, I saw a black bird, possibly a crow or a dark-colored pigeon, perched on the ledge. The white-lace curtains moved as if someone was peering out of the window.

I can't breathe.

S.K. Pierce's Haunt: Haunted Victorian Mansion

GARDNER, MA—Since Rob and Allison Conti purchased and beautifully restored the S.K. Pierce Victorian Mansion in 2015, I've been able to actually walk inside the house that had haunted my dreams for years. In hindsight, I believe Mattie Cornwell was initially shining a postmortem light on a spiritual battle that was terrorizing the spirits still lingering in Gardner's ghost hotel. The woman who was hovering over a man and demanding a confession, however, may not have been Cornwell.

Who was this angry spirit, and why was she saying "Confess" to a shadowy guy who seemed to be cowering in fear?

Joni Mayhan has an idea who the ghostly woman from my dreams could have been, because the spirit also reached out to her. "I had a recurring dream of a woman in what we called the 'Red Room' being attacked by a younger man," Mayhan told me. "He intended to murder her, but someone walked upstairs and interrupted him. In my dream, I thought the woman was Ellen, S.K. Pierce's second wife, and the man was her stepson, Frank."

Yes, Mayhan believes the mystery woman was Ellen Pierce. But why would she say "Confess" over and over?

Mayhan said there was an intense power struggle between Ellen and the oldest son, Frank, after Sylvester died. "Frank actually sued and lost custody of his younger siblings, hoping to gain more control of his father's estate," Mayhan said. "After Sylvester's death in 1888, there were skirmishes between his heirs. Ellen took legal action against her stepson Frank for excessively spending against Sylvester's estate, stating that she was fully capable of handling the probate on her own."

Could the documents that were thrown from the second-floor window be related to the spending habits of Ellen's stepson? Based on one artifact left in the house from her heyday, it's possible. "Her personalized safe still sits in the second-floor landing, a testament to her importance in the household," Mayhan said. "Not many people had safes in the late 1800s, especially not women."

In addition to the familial conflict that Pierce's second wife suffered while living at the Victorian mansion, Mayhan said that she also had a tough time earning the respect from her peers. "Despite joining all the right social clubs, she was always viewed as Pierce's trophy wife due to their thirty-year age difference," she said. "If she tried to fit into the community, she continually failed."

As far as the ghosts still lingering at the S.K. Pierce Victorian Mansion, Mayhan said Ellen's spirit was one of the more dominant figures in the house. "As a medium and paranormal investigator, I've connected with Ellen on many occasions. I've found her to be iron-willed when she needs to be, but also witty and compassionate," Mayhan explained. "I believe she took on a huge role when she married Sylvester and was always at odds with his son, who was only a few years younger than she was."

When I brought up the theory that Pierce's maid, Mattie Cornwell, was possibly hiding a scandalous pregnancy that involved Pierce, Mayhan quickly shot it down. "As we all know, money covered up a lot of sins back in the Victorian era, but I'm not convinced this is the case here," she said. "Rumors have persisted throughout the ages that Mattie had romantic notions regarding her employer, but there is no proof to substantiate it."

Mayhan said Cornwell died at a young age but left an indelible mark on the house. "Her primary focus was caring for the Pierce children. She was firm but loving with the children, keeping them mindful of their manners and helping them grow into the influential men they would one day become," she said.

"Psychic mediums still claim she roams the hallways, but I'm not one of them."

While she believes that Cornwell was crossed over years ago, Mayhan said that the S.K. Pierce Victorian Mansion that she knew well was truly a house of broken dreams. "Despite many good intentions, no one has ever found lasting happiness there," she explained. "The souls trapped inside continue to linger as though they are still searching for the contentment denied to them in life. I hope they eventually find some peace. After everything they've endured, they certainly deserve it."

Crime Q&A: Joni Mayhan

As soon as the house was purchased by Rob and Allison Conti and renovations began in earnest, the hauntings subsided.

—*Joni Mayhan,* Bones in the Basement

Joni Mayhan spent years communicating with the spirits lurking in the shadows of the S.K. Pierce Victorian Mansion in Gardner, Massachusetts. The *Bones in the Basement* author said her interactions with the house's ghostly inhabitants consumed her thoughts for years. "Many of us fell in love with the Victorian

PHOTO COURTESY JONI MAYHAN

138

mansion," she told me. "For me and many others, it almost became an addiction. If we weren't there, we were thinking about it."

Armed with several best-selling books, including *Ghost Magnet* and *Signs of Spirits*, Mayhan said it was tough letting go when she relocated from Massachusetts to Indiana in 2016. "I finally made the decision to break free," she said. "This was only one chapter in my life, and I couldn't allow it to consume me further. Since that time, I've gone back to visit and am thrilled to see it being brought back to its former glory, but I no longer feel the pull to remain there like I did before."

In the interview, Mayhan talks about her connection with a mansion that seemed to have a soul of its own and debunks a few of the myths and misconceptions associated with Gardner's grand dame.

Q: There's so much misinformation regarding the S.K. Pierce Victorian Mansion's backstory. Which one of those myths was the most outlandish?

A: Many stories floated around about the mansion that have no validity. Probably the worst one involved Jay Stemmerman supposedly winning the Victorian in a card game. Through my research, I can see how this mistruth was started. While writing *Bones in the Basement*, I was able to track down the deed to the house and discovered that the purchase price was left blank.

According to Jay's family, he befriended Edward Pierce, who was the current owner, and spent many weekends at the mansion. The house was in bad shape and needed a massive renovation. Jay offered to "buy" the house from Edward and do the necessary work but still allow Edward to live there until he died. At that point, we do know that Stemmerman took ownership of the mansion and invested over $100,000 into the home. It's highly doubtful the house was won during a card game, even though that was a far more enticing story.

Q: I've heard rumors of a prostitute being murdered in the house. Any truth to that story?

A: I too was intrigued by the story of a prostitute being murdered in the mansion, but I couldn't find any hard facts to back it up. According to the coroner reports, the only people who died in the house were members of the Pierce family and Eino Saari, the man who burned to death in the mansion in 1963.

With that said, it's not inconceivable that it happened. The mansion was used as a boardinghouse for many years. While it started out as an upstanding rooming house, it became seedier in its later years, allowing in people from various walks of life. It also sat vacant for nearly thirty years after Jay Stemmerman moved to Florida, and was frequently used by vagrants. It's possible that someone brought a prostitute there, but if she was indeed murdered, her body was removed and dumped in another location, however, I couldn't find verification of that either.

Q: Any idea how the ghost kids ended up in the house?

A: We do know that Edward Pierce's youngest daughter, Rachel, died in the house in 1916 at the age of two years old from gastroenteritis, a very strong bacterial infection. Investigators and psychic mediums have encountered her on numerous occasions. Her voice has been recorded on multiple EVPs, and she could sometimes be encouraged to push a ball across the floor.

Others have encountered the ghost of a young boy. During the period when the Veau family owned the house, they would see him running through the house. One time, the apparition was so clear, Mark Veau thought it was his son until he discovered him sound asleep in his bedroom.

When Edwin and Lillian Gonzalez owned the house, the boy was seen by neighbors running past two of the first-floor windows. Investigators and mediums have confirmed his existence over the years but haven't been able to identify him.

Several mediums felt that he was the son of a servant and died in the house. Many surmise he drowned in the basement cistern because of the heightened activity and EVPs recorded in that area. Others feel he was hit by a car near the property and drifted in to join the ghostly ranks.

Q: Based on your research, are there any reports of unnatural deaths or murder in the S.K. Pierce Victorian?

A: I wasn't able to find any unnatural deaths at the mansion. The only death that comes close is the death of Eino Saari. At the time, rumors persisted that he died of spontaneous combustion, but we've since debunked these rumors. Eino was a heavy drinker and a smoker. It's highly likely he spilled moonshine on his clothing and then fell asleep with a lit cigarette, resulting in his death.

Q: You've been able to go inside several times since the renovations. What are your thoughts now about the house?

A: The Victorian is still haunted, but it's far more congenial. Any lingering negative energy is long gone, and the ghosts seem content now. I believe that most of the hauntings experienced by Edwin and Lillian came from a combination of factors. While they owned the house, they allowed unmonitored paranormal groups to investigate on a weekly basis. While most of the investigators were ethical in their methods, several others weren't and relied on provocation to get better results.

The other factor that contributed to the extensive hauntings was the fact that the house wasn't being renovated. It was crumbling bit by bit and wouldn't have lasted many more years without the substantial funds needed to restore it. As soon as the house was purchased by Rob and Allison Conti and renovations began in earnest, the hauntings subsided. The current caretakers still often have paranormal experiences, but they are far more subdued than they were in the past.

The Forgotten

Unidentified Female Body Found Race Point Dunes July 26, 1974.
—Lady of the Dunes's gravestone

The Lady of the Dunes is the nickname for an unidentified woman discovered on July 26, 1974, in the Race Point Dunes, Provincetown, Massachusetts.

Cape Cod's Provincetown

When I write my historical-based books, I spend months and sometimes years researching the ghost lore associated with a city or town before I even pitch the book to my publisher. I also let the "ghosts" guide me, so I allow my intuition to summon me to the sites covered in the book at first. Sometimes my gut leads me into extremely scary situations, which was the case with *Wicked Salem: Exploring Lingering Lore and Legends.*

Cape Cod's Provincetown? It's a different kind of creepy.

"Provincetown is equally as haunted as Salem, but the spirits aren't as pissed off," I told Solaris BlueRaven on her weekly podcast, *Ravenstar's Witching Hour.* "There's a dark contemporary history in Provincetown compared to Salem. It was a playground for serial killers, mobsters, and underground activity from the 1950s to the 1970s. It's literally the tip of the world. It's the easternmost point of Cape Cod, so it has an end-of-the-world vibe to it. People who want to get away gravitate to Provincetown. A lot of creative types, like Tennessee Williams and Eugene O'Neill, went there to be inspired. It has beautiful beaches, and its overall vibe is magical . . . but it's also very haunted."

I talked about how ghost lore was part of the vernacular of Salem. In Provincetown, year-round locals admit that the town is extremely active with spirits, but they're wary to go on the record and give the lowdown about their ghostly encounters. "What happens in Provincetown stays in Provincetown, and that's the case with its ghost lore as well," I joked on BlueRaven's radio show.

Known as the spot where Pilgrims first set foot on Cape Cod on November 21, 1620, before signing the Mayflower Compact, it's no surprise that Provincetown is a town full of secrets and spirits.

"After spending some time in Provincetown, one can come to feel that all of its time-honored public buildings and historic homes are loaded with ghosts," surmised *Cape Encounters*. "The eccentric quality of the town, its maritime location, the ramshackle layout of its structures, and its remote bittersweet atmosphere combine to create the impression of a hamlet permeated with supernatural energy."

Ashley Shakespeare, a veteran ghost tour guide and regular Provincetown drag illusionist, agrees. "Provincetown has always been Bohemian, artistic, and off the beaten path," he explained. "Spirits there, I feel, are the same way. While you may not know their names, you know they are there. Just like vacationers know that the kid who plays the piano at town hall will be there when they come back year after year. They don't know their names but know that they are there."

Shakespeare continued: "It's the same with the spirit world in Provincetown. They may not have any significant ties with any history or great events, but they are existing in their Bohemian, off-the-beaten-path world."

Ghosts with personalities? Shakespeare said his interactions with the spirit realm are similar to his encounters with the living.

"You become friends with people because you understand them and they entertain you for various reasons. I feel spirits do the same thing," he said. "They make themselves known to people because they want fellowship."

Shakespeare said he has been sensitive to the paranormal world for most of his life. He was raised in Manhattan and spent his formative years in Provincetown before moving to Revere. "Growing up, I always felt surrounded by a certain energy I couldn't explain, and I knew most people couldn't or wouldn't understand it. I spent a lot of time alone as a child. I was very shy and wasn't involved in a lot of activities boys my age were. I often felt misunderstood, and I feel that the spirits that surrounded me felt the same way," Shakespeare remembered. "It hasn't changed much in my adult life except I'm more in tune with and have found a certain way to communicate with some spirits that want to make themselves known to me," he continued.

As far as communicating with the spirit realm, Shakespeare said he usually has a physical reaction when a ghost is nearby. "I get chills and goosebumps," he explained. "Every hair on my body stands up. I also have been physically touched by spirits and have seen them open doors, turn on TVs, and play with my pets."

Provincetown's most haunted? Shakespeare said the Atlantic House and Route 6 because "many people have died on that road," adding that many decades ago, "Long Point was the 'bad side of town' with pirates, gypsies, gambling, and prostitutes," he explained. "With that cast of characters, you can imagine the goings-on that occurred. Also, there are a number of houses that were floated over from Long Point as the shorelines started to recede."

For the record, Long Point was a thriving village from 1818 through the late 1850s. Residents, mainly fishermen, who called the extreme tip of Cape Cod home, inexplicably decided to abandon the thin strip of land. One by one, they painstakingly floated their homes across the harbor. By the end of the Civil War, only two houses remained. The Long Point Light, built in 1827, stands as an eerie sentinel of what is now a ghost town. Historians are stumped as to what truly inspired the mass migration. Theories range from the lack of fresh water to proliferation of sharks.

However, Shakespeare believes the exodus was fueled by something more sinister.

He said the spirits from Long Point's nineteenth-century heyday continue to haunt the structures they once inhabited. "For the most part, my relationships and interactions with the spirits in Ptown were the same as with those in the living world. We shared the same little town, glanced at each other as we went about our day," Shakespeare said, adding that there was one exception. "She was a mischievous eight-year-old girl. I lived in one of the floaters from Long Point in the West End on Atwood Lane." Shakespeare believes the girl was killed, possibly crushed to death, when the house was moved to the West End.

"She was what you would think an eight-year-old little girl would be: inquisitive, mischievous, and liked to play," he said. "She would unlock and open the kitchen door. I would wake up to find my TV on, and the channel was changed to a station that I never knew I had, never mind watched. She also used to play with the cats and dog, keeping them and herself entertained."

The former Provincetown year-rounder continued: "It was almost like having another little sister. I actually miss her sometimes, and whenever I go to Ptown, I walk by the house and say hello to her." Shakespeare said the spirits of Provincetown, including the mischievous ghost girl, don't creep him out. "The spirit world doesn't scare me," he responded. "Certain spirits may spook me from time to time, but I'm never scared. I've embraced the spirit world, and I feel once you embrace something, it doesn't scare you any longer."

His advice to visitors looking for a ghost adventure? "When in Ptown, go with the flow," he continued. "It's home to some and vacation paradise to others . . . both the living and the dead. Bask in the residual spirit energy . . . and consider it a gift to you from the ghosts of Provincetown."

Cape Cod's Haunt: Unitarian Universalist Meetinghouse

PROVINCETOWN, MA—Used as an infirmary during the flu epidemic of 1918, the Unitarian Universalist Meetinghouse (UUMH) was built in 1847 and is reportedly one of Provincetown's more paranormally active locations. "People say that they've seen a woman in full Colonial garb walking across the sanctuary," explained Adam Berry from *Kindred Spirits*. "They also hear singing when no one is there. When I was doing a fundraiser in the building one night, I heard distinct footsteps walk across the church's pulpit."

Other sources, like *Uncommon Sense Media*, have echoed Berry's observation that UUMH is indeed active. "It meets all the criteria for being a haunted house because it's an old building and it has a creepy history. Like all haunted houses, people report seeing 'something' moving from the corner of their eye and also 'felt a presence' when alone."

Formerly called the Universalist Church of the Redeemer, the striking white structure located at 236 Commercial Street was the crown jewel of Provincetown's spiritual community. "Every detail of the beautiful Christopher Wren tower and the façade, with its dignified simplicity with the great spruces on either side, make an unforgettable picture," reported *New Beacon* in 1962. "Inside the church is the same beautiful sanctuary, just as it was in 1847, when it was built, with the same priceless Sandwich glass chandeliers."

The structure's acoustics are to die for and oddly accentuate the church's more notorious spirits: singing specters.

The Unitarian Universalist Meetinghouse is "notable for having a ghostly choir," confirmed *Cape Encounters*. According to the account, the building's historian was alone downstairs in the meetinghouse when she claimed to have heard the ghost group singing. "She waited ten minutes before daring to walk upstairs to confirm the source. When she reached the top of the stairs, she found the second floor quiet and empty."

The church's former sexton, Oscar, had a face-to-face encounter with the ghostly choir. "His memory included recollections of looking up and seeing the ensemble dressed in coats," *Cape Encounters* continued.

So, why a ghost choir?

One theory is that the ghosts of the Commercial Street haunt are somehow tied to the Great Pandemic of 1918. The plague started in Boston on August 27, when several sailors were stricken with a deadly flu virus. In three days, there were 58 cases in Boston, and it quickly spread to 2,000 people within two weeks.

"This epidemic started about four weeks ago and has developed so rapidly that the camp is demoralized and all ordinary work is held up till it has passed," reported a beleaguered physician from nearby Camp Devens. "These men start with what appears to be an ordinary attack of influenza and when brought to the hospital they very rapidly develop the most viscous type of pneumonia that has ever been seen. Two hours after admission they have the mahogany spots over the cheekbones, and a few hours later you can begin to see the cyanosis extending from their ears and spreading all over the face. It is only a matter of a few hours then until death comes, and it is simply a struggle for air until they suffocate. It is horrible."

The killer flu quickly traveled to Provincetown, and locals felt under siege. "In 1918 came the flu epidemic. Then Provincetown put on a strange face," wrote Mary Heaton Vorse in *A Time and the Town: A Provincetown Chronicle*. "Everyone went around masked with an antiseptic cloth. It made one feel that the days of pestilence in the Middle Ages had returned. People were stricken so fast that hospitals couldn't care for them. A hospital was improvised in the Universalist Church."

In Provincetown, more than 829 cases of the deadly "Spanish flu" killed more than 45,000 people in Massachusetts over a four-month period. According to Vorse, at least 25 died at the Universalist Church.

Eyewitnesses who have encountered the ghost choir said they've seen around two dozen apparitions in this ghostly chorus.

Based on reports, it's possible that these spirited songbirds are a residual haunting from the pandemic flu era. Oddly, the numbers of those who died at the church correlate to the spirits participating in the ghost-choir ensemble.

And what about the female apparition wearing Colonial garb? One idea is that she's just passing through, which is common for an energy not bound to a specific location. Another possibility is that she's linked to the *Mayflower*. Dorothy Bradford drowned on December 7, 1620, in Provincetown Harbor. Legend suggests it was a depression-induced suicide. However, it's more likely that she accidentally fell off the vessel into the freezing harbor while her husband, William Bradford, was searching for suitable land to build a colony. The spot where the meetinghouse currently resides was marshland in the 1600s, and it's possible that the Colonial-era woman washed ashore in the present-day vicinity of the church.

CRIME PROFILE: SANDRA LEE

> Let's try to give this woman a name. Everybody deserves a
> name on their headstone.
> —Sandra Lee, *The Shanty*

It's the cold case that has haunted Provincetown for more than forty-five years. The Lady of the Dunes's severely mutilated corpse was found on a secluded service road near Dunes' Edge Campground at Race Point Beach on July 26, 1974. On the day the body was discovered, the buzzing insects sounded like muted screams, alluding to the horrors that unfolded in the wooded area almost half a century ago.

The ghost of Provincetown's most infamous gone girl has haunted Sandra Lee, author of *The Shanty* and a Provincetown regular since the 1970s. The crime writer was only nine years old when she claimed to have stumbled on the cold case of the century. According to Lee, the Lady of the Dunes's decomposing

body continues to haunt her dreams. During an emotional discussion that stirred up childhood demons, Lee told me that the woman's dead body sounded like a string of pearls rubbing together.

"She was in the brush, in the seagrass about fifteen feet from an access road," Lee recalled. "The road follows the backside of Dunes' Edge Campground. She was in the thick of the brush. It was nothing shy of horrific. It was something I will never forget."

Lee, who camped at Dunes' Edge every July in the early 1970s, said it has taken her years to talk publicly about the horrors from her childhood. While there is a local teenage girl on record who is credited with calling responding officers to the scene in 1974, the author said she and her sister found the rotting corpse of the Lady of the Dunes two days before police were alerted.

"I stumbled down an incline with my dog," she continued. "The dog was ahead of me. My dog got excited about something. I heard a very strange noise. If you could imagine someone holding a string of pearls, I heard that sound. And then there was a horrible smell. At first, I attributed it to low tide," said Lee with emotion as she recollected the horrific scene. "She was face down. Her hair was a mess, and I could see a gouge in the right side of her neck. Her arms were tucked down in the sand, so I didn't know anything was missing. I recognized the green blanket right away. The lower half of her body was covered with something."

Lee said the horrible sound has stayed with her for years. "It wasn't until much later that I realized that the sound of someone playing with a pearl necklace was from the maggots," she said. "Her body was covered with maggots. I believe there were a few people who found the body, but there is only one who spoke to police in person about it."

On July 26, 1974, a girl who was walking her dog discovered the naked decomposing body of a woman in her twenties or early thirties. The body was lying face down wearing Wrangler jeans with a blue bandana placed crudely under her head. A green blanket was also found at the scene. The murder victim had long auburn or reddish-colored hair clamped in a glittery, elastic-band ponytail and was approximately five-foot-six inches tall. She had an athletic build and was approximately 135 pounds. The Lady of the Dunes, as she has been nicknamed, had extensive dental work done on her teeth, worth thousands of dollars. The killer had removed several of the teeth—a practice that James "Whitey" Bulger and his cronies were known for. Her hands had been removed, and she had been nearly decapitated with what is believed to have been a military entrenching tool. She had also received massive trauma to the side of her skull. Police believed she had been sexually assaulted.

Oddly, the gruesome crime scene became the single most-visited tourist attraction in Provincetown during its peak season in the summer of 1974.

Provincetown became a safe haven for lesbians and gay men in the late 1960s and early 1970s. There were several LGBT-friendly bars, including the Atlantic House or A-House, which "turned gay" in 1976, the Pilgrim House, Ptown's earliest drag bar called Weathering Heights, the Moors, and of course, the Crown & Anchor.

Lee reminisced about the early 1970s with fondness. "Before 1974, I remember drinking out of glass Coke bottles and eating candy apples," she said, adding that there was a dark side to the town's picturesque facade. "It wasn't fun for me after 1974. In the 1970s, Provincetown was a huge port for money, drugs, and human trafficking. Whitey had a history of bisexuality. Gay-related crimes were often overlooked in the 1970s. At the time, people weren't onto Whitey's trips to Provincetown. It was his playground, and no one knew he was doing half of the things he was doing here. It was the perfect place for the disposal of the body."

Lee said her stepfather, a violent alcoholic, would spend nights at the Crown & Anchor with Bulger while her family camped at Dunes' Edge. "Not many people knew that Bulger was hanging out in Provincetown, nor did they realize he was a switch hitter," Lee said. "My stepfather would stumble into the campsite during the wee morning hours. He was always inebriated and disheveled, often bruised and bloody, and sometimes wearing a green cotton blanket around his shoulders, which he'd taken from the inn."

The author said that she fears her stepfather may have been at the scene, as he often interacted with Bulger in Milton and Provincetown. "Whether it was my stepfather, I don't know. It was too coincidental that we camped there. If you rolled off the embankment, there she was," Lee said. "The reason why I found her was because I was running from a bad situation. Finding her certainly put things in perspective for me because obviously she was in a much worse situation. In a sense, she helped save my life. Coming from an abusive home environment, I thought this was as bad as it gets. But, when you stumbled on what I did, you realized that what happened to the Lady of the Dunes is as bad as it gets."

The Provincetown Police Department (PPD) claimed in previous interviews that several witnesses and photographs have placed Bulger in the area at the time of the murder. However, Lee responded, saying, "Nothing concrete has yet tied Bulger to the Provincetown murder, but he has not yet been ruled out as a suspect." The PPD followed up on several initial leads that pointed to local individuals as well as two serial killers, including Tony "Chop Chop" Costa. However, the notorious murderer committed suicide in 1970. The theories were all proven wrong.

Bulger was captured in Santa Monica, California, after more than sixteen years on the run. Fleeing Boston in 1995, he was charged with participating in nineteen murders as well as a slew of other horrific crimes. Stephen "the Rifleman" Flemmi, testified in federal court that Bulger lured twenty-six-year-old Deborah Hussey to a South Boston home in 1985. Flemmi claimed that Bulger strangled her. Following the trial, Bulger was sentenced to two consecutive terms of life in prison.

Bulger, who was in a wheelchair, was found dead on October 30, 2018, at the age of eighty-nine. He was fatally assaulted using a grisly "lock-in-the-sock" by inmates and killed within hours of his arrival at Hazelton Penitentiary in West Virginia.

Did Bulger and his cronies kill the Lady of the Dunes? Lee believed she was possibly one of the South Boston gang's victims. However, her main motivation is to find closure for the unidentified woman.

Lee wrote a fictionalized account in 2011 about the Lady of the Dunes case, called *The Shanty*, while camping at Dunes' Edge Campground. "It was terribly difficult for me to write. I wrote about the case in fictional form because technically it was still a pending investigation. It was difficult for me to write because I had to revisit a lot of demons I thought I left behind," she said. "In the long run, it was extremely cathartic for me. It was tough, but I tried to stay focused. I needed to go through so much healing before even writing this book."

Lee said the woman would appear in her dreams while she camped at Dunes' Edge Campground, implying that the woman's restless spirit still lingers in the area.

More than four decades after her murder, a metal casket in Provincetown's St. Peter's Cemetery contains the remains of the Lady of the Dunes. The gravestone is labeled as "unidentified female," and it's falling apart.

The author hopes detectives at the PPD can at least identify the murdered woman. "Let's remember her," Lee emoted. "We're running out of time. Let's try to give this woman a name. Everybody deserves a name on their headstone. Keeping her in the forefront of the public eye will help solve this case. The only way to do it is to keep the story alive."

Fall River Cult Murders

The so-called Bridgewater Triangle, an area of about 200 square miles in southeastern Massachusetts, is the epicenter of the commonwealth's alleged paranormal activity and over-the-top urban legends. Tales associated with the Triangle include: Native American curses; satanic cults; a red-headed hitchhiker; a swamp called Hockomock, which the Wampanoag tribe believed was "the place where spirits dwell"; numerous UFO sightings, including one as far back as 1760; three-foot cryptids known as Pukwudgies; and the Assonet Ledge in Freetown State Forest, where visitors report seeing ghosts standing, jumping, and inexplicably disappearing.

Of all the hocus pocus occurring on the spooky South Coast, the most spine-tingling story about the Bridgewater Triangle is the real-life horror that unfolded in Freetown State Forest in November 1978. The decomposed body of Mary-Lou Arruda, a teen cheerleader from nearby Raynham, was discovered tied to a tree in the forest. The murdered girl was fifteen years old. She disappeared in the afternoon of September 8, 1978. A newspaper delivery boy found her bicycle near the scene. She had been missing for two months.

James M. Kater, a then thirty-two-year-old donut maker from Brockton, was indicted in connection with the Arruda murder. His green car was spotted in Raynham, and his vehicle had a nine-inch gash in the front that matched the girl's bicycle. He was also on probation for a similar incident in 1968, when he kidnapped a girl from Andover. Kater has stood trial four times, and his final appeal was rejected by the U.S. Supreme Court in 2007. He died as a prisoner of the state at Lemuel Shattuck Hospital on January 9, 2016.

Former Raynham selectman Don McKinnon referred to Kater as "evil encased in a human body" in an article published in the *Enterprise* newspaper announcing his death on January 26, 2016. "If he had not been caught by the Raynham police, I believe he had all the markings of a serial killer," McKinnon told the *Enterprise*. "I'm sure if they didn't catch him, he would have gone on to do this sort of thing on a regular basis. But if you try to figure out why he did what he did, it's beyond reason."

According to trial documents, "Arruda had been alive and in a standing position when she was tied to the tree." Once she became unconscious, the weight of her head against the ligature around her neck caused her to suffocate. While there are no ties between her murder and the alleged reports of satanic cult activity in Freetown State Forest, the case reinforced the idea that the area was cursed.

"The Town of Freetown was purchased in 1659 from the Wampanoag tribe and the town was incorporated in 1683. The Native Americans believed the land was highly sacred when Wamsutta sold it, possibly without the backing of the tribe, maybe the cause of the evil energy," reported the SouthCoast Ghost paranormal group online. "Many believe that the events of the area have turned the once-gentle spirits violent, attracting evil to it and the forest in return is being fed by the evil. Native Americans claim the horrible crimes and hauntings will not stop until the tribe is given back the land."

People who stumble on the location where Arruda's body was found say it's paranormally active. "I have seen shadow people," reported an anonymous paranormal investigator on the *Unexplained Mysteries* forum. "I have seen a spirit of a girl near the site where they found Mary Lou Arruda's body in 1978. I recently spent the entire night in the forest with my group. We had some people feel like they were pushed. We heard laughter in the woods. Occasionally, we heard groans, breathing, and screams." The source reported seeing lights like softball-sized fireflies at the top of the trees. "One from our group swore she saw someone jumping from tree to tree, but it was unverified."

Another source on *Unexplained Mysteries* echoed claims about the negative energy associated with the forest. "I had the distinct feeling that we were being followed and watched," he confirmed. "I could have sworn I saw people in the woods."

One year after the Arruda murder, all hell broke loose in the cursed Freetown State Forest. Karen Marsden, a woman believed to be a prostitute in Fall River, was savagely killed. Carl Drew, a self-proclaimed devil worshipper and pimp, reportedly led ritualistic gatherings in the forest at a place known as the Ice Shack. The so-called "son of Satan" was also accused of three cult-like murders and was allegedly the leader of the devil-worshiping prostitution ring.

"Drew was on trial for the February 1980 murder of Karen Marsden, a Fall River prostitute whose skull and other remains were found in a wooded area of Westport in April the same year," reported *SouthCoast Today*. "While on trial for Marsden's murder, he was also under indictment for the October 1979 killing of Doreen Levesque, another Fall River prostitute."

Robin Murphy, then a young sex worker who testified against Drew, claimed the man organized several satanic gatherings, which led to three ritualistic murders. "At the trial, Murphy said that she, Drew and two others had driven Marsden to a wooded area of Westport where they got out of the car and Murphy began dragging Marsden through the woods by her throat and hair," explained *SouthCoast Today*. "Drew told Marsden to give Murphy a ring she was wearing but she refused so Drew cut her finger off to get it."

Murphy, who claimed to have been possessed by Satan, said she slit Marsden's throat because the cult leader demanded it. Murphy testified that Drew carved an "X" in the murdered woman's chest and started speaking in a demonic tongue. He then dabbed the mutilated woman's blood on his fingers and marked an "X" on Murphy's forehead, telling her that the sacrifice was an initiation into his cult. Murphy said two other murders, including the savage slaughter of Levesque, were eerily similar.

Séances using the skulls of the victims were supposedly held in a Black Mass ritual, according to Murphy, in the Freetown State Forest. "The killing of Doreen Levesque was an offering of the soul to Satan and so was the killing of Miss Marsden," Murphy said to the court. Drew is still in prison for the murders he was accused of inciting three decades ago.

Murphy, whose testimony helped convict Drew and another man, Andrew Maltais, who died in prison, was eventually convicted of second-degree murder and sentenced to life in prison.

After several hearings, Murphy was denied parole even after she claimed that she didn't participate in the satanic-style murder of her former lover, Marsden.

"Robin was the mastermind in all three homicides and manipulated everyone," said Representative Alan Silvia, Fall River's state legislator, during the March 2017 parole hearing. Silvia is a former police detective.

Inspired by the Fall River Cult Murders case, Freetown State Forest became a hotbed of Black Mass gatherings in the 1980s. One man, William LaFrance, was found camping in the forest with rows of yellow candles and satanic symbols carved in the dirt. Officers found "666" tacked to the tree near LaFrance's car. Park rangers claimed that the haunted Assonet Ledge was also plagued with freshly painted satanic symbols, skulls, and pentagrams in the late 1980s. For the record, visitors still claim to encounter spirits at the abandoned quarry, which is believed to be the site of multiple suicides over the years.

The ranger station, a cabin-like structure built in the 1940s for loggers in the forest, is where a lot of the cult activity is believed to have taken place. People who claimed to have seen the wooden structure said it's where Carl Drew held his infamous drug-induced séances. Animal bones have been found in the area near the hijacked shack. There's also a structure known as the "Ice Shack," but it's commonly mistaken for the ranger station.

There was also a bunker in the Freetown State Forest. Rangers found pentagrams and evidence of ritualistic gatherings in the culvert-style cave. Officers believed the bunker was evil. However, former members of the Society of Creative Anachronism (SCA) claimed it was a gathering spot for neo-pagan and Wiccan practitioners and not followers of the devil.

In addition to all the alleged cult activity, a ghostly trucker has been spotted regularly on Copicut Road in the heart of Freetown State Forest. He supposedly blares his horn and threatens passing motorists who venture into the forest at night.

Whether Freetown State Forest is actually haunted or not, there's no denying its freakishly macabre history. As someone who has spent time in the forest, I can confirm there's definitely an eerie electricity that permeates the 5,217-acre area. There was a massive fire in the woods in March 1976 that damaged 500 acres and another in September 1980 that destroyed 230 acres.

In addition to the murders in the late 1970s, more deaths occurred, including that of a drifter who was killed in 1987 after being mistaken as an undercover police officer. Two men were shot to death on Bell Rock Road in 2001, and there were two assaults in 1991 and 1998.

Rachel Hoffman from Paranormal Xpeditions produced a documentary on Freetown in 2014 for her *True Crime Paranormal* series. The veteran ghost hunter said the serene forest turned nightmarish after dark. The Bay State's most haunted forest? Hoffman believes the Freetown State Forest is a hotbed of primordial evil. It's almost as if the forest somehow devours its victims.

"It wasn't hard for us to see how bodies could be hidden for three to six months at a time," Hoffman said. "The forest is extremely dense and the drop-offs are extremely high. The highway goes in all different directions. If you were a victim, I don't know how you would escape the clutches of a murderer out there. It seems like the forest could swallow you . . . and it has to."

But is it haunted? Absolutely. It's as if the Freetown State Forest has a devilish mind of its own.

CULT'S HAUNT: FREETOWN STATE FOREST

ASSONET, MA—There's no denying the "something wicked this way comes" vibe as demonologist James Annitto and I headed into the heart of the Freetown State Forest during the summer of 2019. With Annitto's son in the backseat of his vehicle, we passed by the site on Copicut Road where teenaged kidnap victim Mary Lou Arruda was tied to a tree and died more than three decades ago in a senseless murder that continues to haunt the South Coast.

We parked in a clearing near Bell Rock Road and started to walk down a dirt path known as the Upper Ledge. As we proceeded to hike down a dusty trail leading to the supposedly haunted Freetown Ledge, Annitto and his son were eager to explore the wooded area that some view as cursed land.

Not me. Compared to my enthusiastic travel companions, I was a bit more apprehensive. There was an inexplicable energy that was unsettling to me. Something didn't feel right.

My wariness could have been attributed to the fact that the Old Catholic Church deacon and I were getting attacked by a swarm of locust-like insects as soon as we started to walk down the unpaved Upper Ledge road. "I truly don't know if they were locusts," Annitto told me after our adventure when I asked him about the flying bugs. "I even had one fly right at me. Locusts symbolize God's wrath, so maybe it was a sign to leave and not enter the forest. But locusts were also said to be the love of God because John the Baptist sustained off of locusts and honey. Whatever they were, it was definitely a bizarre experience."

I asked Annitto if he thought Freetown State Forest was cursed. "It's possible," he responded. "The one thing you notice while you are in the area is that it's a reservation as well. Native Americans used to linger and live within the areas we were walking and still have stuff to do with the land today."

The noted demonologist said that he had heard of many strange tales of the unexplained coming from the Bridgewater Triangle region. "There are many legends that relate to Freetown State Forest in the sense that the white men took over, and the Native Americans cursed the land as a payback of sorts for taking over their land by force," Annitto told me. "I can't really say if the land is cursed or not, but I've definitely heard of a lot of experiences within the Freetown State Forest and surrounding areas. In fact, just north of the forest is Hockomock Swamp, and it's said to be cursed as well."

In his book *Dark Woods*, Christopher Balzano weighs in on the Native American legends associated with the Freetown State Forest. "There are several stories of burial grounds covered over in the forest," Balzano wrote. "Another motif is the appearance of phantoms seen as lights or orbs. In Wampanoag legend, there is the Tei-Pai-Wankas, which are said to be the spirits of people who passed. Full-bodied spirits are sometimes seen looking lost or confused or reenacting the tragedy that happened."

What actually went down four centuries ago? "The area was possibly the site of Native American massacres at the hands of the

Puritans," posted Peter Muise on his New England Folklore blog. "It also sits inside the Bridgewater Triangle, an area notorious for paranormal phenomena."

According to Muise, the spirit activity seems to intensify in the area near Assonet Ledge. "Some visitors claim to have seen ghosts of Native Americans walking in the trees near the cliff," he wrote, adding that the legend implies that the Wampanoag and Narragansett warriors jumped from the ledge and committed suicide to avoid being killed by the English colonists.

While the legends seem far-fetched because the quarry surrounding the ledge didn't exist in the seventeenth century, Muise believes there's something unnerving about the area. "Much of the land in the Freetown State Forest is actually a Wampanoag reservation, so there is an authentic Native American connection. Perhaps the ghosts died in some other way?"

Muise said there's another story involving a woman with a broken heart. "Many years ago, a young man and woman were deeply in love," he wrote. "They would meet secretly at the ledge at night because their families disapproved of their love. One night the woman arrived at the ledge and waited for her beau. She waited that night, but he never came. In despair, she threw herself off the ledge to her death in the cold water."

In addition to the legends associated with Assonet Ledge, there's a site called Profile Rock that looks like a man's face carved in a granite outcropping. Lore suggested that it was the face of the great Native American sachem, Chief Massasoit, leader of the Wampanoag people. He's responsible for saving the Pilgrims in Plymouth from starvation by offering corn to the dying settlers.

Sadly, the rock formation that resembled the chief's profile collapsed a few weeks before my visit to the Freetown State Forest with my demonologist friend in August 2019.

Annitto told me that it would make sense that the spirit activity would intensify if there were unmarked graves or an unreported massacre in the woods. "Native Americans have been known to do protection rituals on their lands in a spiritual sense," he explained. "If there was battle or conflict, these protections could have been activated, especially when outsiders step onto these very sacred lands."

Based on cases that he has worked on in the past, Annitto believes that the spirits at Freetown State Forest could be elemental in nature. "These spirits are intelligent," he said. "They watch your next step and will react depending on your intent."

I mentioned to Annitto that there have been reports of pagan rituals frequently happening in Freetown State Forest. Why would these groups be attracted to this location?

"Many believe that areas like the forest, where there's a high amount of spirit activity, that the veil between the living and the dead is the thinnest. It's what people call portals," he told me. "Not all of these rituals are meant to be bad. Some are for healing and others are considered root magic."

However, the darker ceremonies like the Black Mass animal and possibly human sacrifices held by Carl Drew and his followers in the 1980s may have conjured something inhuman in the woods. "There have been talks about satanic and blood rituals being done within the grounds of the forest. This is a bad idea," he warned. "The ritual may actually conjure something and, because of the heightened activity that already occurs in the forest, it's possible that an inhuman entity could be summoned."

In Henry Scammell's book *Mortal Remains*, the author described the Black Mass rituals allegedly held in the Freetown State Forest in the late 1970s and early 1980s. Goats or stray cats would be slaughtered, and the blood was used to mock Christian baptisms. During the ceremonies, the congregants would supposedly speak in tongues.

"[Satan appears] in a form where we feel his presence, or he takes possession of one of us," claimed Maureen "Sonny" Sparda in *Mortal Remains*. "You can tell when Satan is there. Some people even let him speak through them, in his own language. It isn't human speech; there's no way anyone on earth could fake it."

Another young follower of Drew, nicknamed Cookie, claimed that the Fall River cult also sacrificed humans. "They kill every thirty days or so—on the full moon," she told police in the early 1980s and was quoted in Scammell's *Mortal Remains* book. "It's always a ritual, that they offer up the victim as a sacrifice to Satan."

These alleged sacrifices were held at night on a flat-stone slab deep in the woods. As Annitto and I walked near a clearing that could have been used for these Black Mass ceremonies, I asked him about the alarming number of animals that have reportedly been ritualistically sacrificed in Freetown State Forest over the years. "In the days before Christianity, goats were killed and then burned as an offering to God. These types of offerings have been practiced by many beliefs and faiths throughout time. The animal sacrifices could be pagan rituals or they could be used for something more sinister. In the same way an offering could be positive, it could also be negative and used to cause harm."

Speaking of a positive offering, Annitto left some tobacco on a rock as a gift for the Native American spirits who seemed to be watching us along the way. Why tobacco? "Native Americans bartered in their times and favored tobacco," he told me after we made the trek home. "I wanted to give a peace offering in exchange for our safety and ease of mind. We were intruders on their land, and even though we were there with no negative intent, the tobacco symbolized those peaceful intentions."

Yes, Annitto has done this sort of thing in the past. "I've used this before on cases with supposed hostile Native American spirits in similar locations," he explained. "It helped quiet the activity, and they realized that we didn't mean them harm."

Apparently, the demonologist's tobacco offering worked. We managed to make it safely back to the car after hiking for hours down long, winding paths without a cell phone connection. Luckily, the locust-like bugs stopped attacking us as we headed back.

Nope, we didn't have a *Blair Witch Project* kind of a day. But it could have been.

In hindsight, Annitto wasn't surprised that people have reportedly gotten lost while exploring the Freetown State Forest. "I thought it was beautiful and of course huge," he told me. "We could have kept walking and never found our way back. Even though it's really close to Fall River, it was like we traveled back in time."

James "Whitey" Bulger

There's no denying the sick-and-twisted legacy left in South Boston by notorious mob boss James "Whitey" Bulger, but were there any signs from his youth that he was a monster in the making?

His last words, written to a friend with whom he corresponded from his prison cell in Florida, suggested he was bad to the bloody end. "Don't worry about me," Bulger wrote in February 2018. "I'm too mean to die."

Bulger was beaten to death by two inmates eight months after penning the letter published by the *Boston Globe* on May 14, 2019. He was eighty-nine. "A batch of Bulger's prison letters, made available to the *Globe*, offer fresh insight into Bulger's state of mind—by turns, wry, emotional, and bitter—as he neared the end," wrote reporter Shelley Murphy. "They also offer a chronicle of how his health was deteriorating in solitary confinement at a penitentiary in Florida, an account which, if accurate, contradicts the authorities who claimed his condition had dramatically improved, making him eligible for a transfer to the prison in West Virginia where he was murdered."

Bulger had a reputation of being cruel and, based on his rough childhood, he seemed to be in trouble from the beginning. Born on September 3, 1929, in Dorchester, Massachusetts, Bulger moved to the projects in South Boston after his father lost his arm in an industrial accident. As a teenager, he was known to instigate violent fights and steal cars. He soon graduated to more serious crimes and spent nine years in prison in the 1950s after spearheading a string of bank robberies in Indiana and Rhode Island. He was sentenced to federal prison and was transferred to Alcatraz, off the coast of San Francisco, California, after he supposedly tried to escape.

He earned the nickname "Whitey" from local police because of his blond hair. He actually loathed the moniker and preferred "Jimmy" or "Boots," the name locals gave him because of his penchant for wearing cowboy boots. No surprise based on his history of sadism, but it's said that he hid a switchblade in his country-style shoes when he roamed the streets of Southie.

One theory that could have contributed to Bulger's downward spiral during his formative years was that he struggled with his sexual orientation and responded to the inner turmoil by attacking others.

In 2006, author and radio icon Howie Carr dropped a bombshell in his book *The Brothers Bulger*, claiming that Bulger "got his start in the criminal underworld as a teen after a lesbian pimp recruited him to hustle out of gay bars." "According to survivors of the era, Whitey worked out of a couple of gay bars on Stuart Street, primarily a joint called Mario's, which was also known as the Sail Aweigh. As a young male hustler, he quickly became adept at rolling his tricks—his police record indicates an arrest for 'unarmed robbery' on March 18, 1947. Another of his favorite pickup spots was the Punch Bowl, which was frequently raided by the vice squad. . . .

Whitey may have been hustling to raise some spending money, but he never was exclusively homosexual."

Rumors of Bulger's possible bisexuality surfaced in 2001 after former Boston police superintendent Bob Hayden told the *Boston Herald* he encountered the sociopathic killer at the legendary gay bar in Boston's Bay Village, Jacques. "I'm going back maybe twenty-five years," Hayden told the *Herald*. "I was doing a night detail at Jacques." Hayden claimed Bulger was sitting at the bar, now known for its drag performances, and they chatted. "I've always thought it [Jacques] was perfect for him to lose himself," Hayden said, "to have a few beers undetected."

Did Bulger's issues with his sexual orientation cause him to snap? Yes, it could have been a contributing factor. However, reporters who have followed Bulger's rise as an Irish-American organized crime boss and FBI informant believe he went over the deep end in 1973.

He had a twelve-year relationship with Lindsey Cyr, a waitress and former model from North Weymouth, and they reportedly had a son together. The six-year-old boy died of a severe reaction to aspirin called Reye syndrome. The death of his child, Douglas, tore Bulger apart emotionally.

"It was very difficult for Jimmy because, no matter what, there was nothing that could save this," Cyr told WHDH-TV on June 27, 2011. "Money didn't matter. His power didn't matter." According to Cyr, Bulger felt helpless for the first time in his life. "I'm never going to hurt like this again," Bulger told his girlfriend.

The mob boss was murdered in prison on October 30, 2018.

BULGER'S HAUNT: TRIPLE O'S

SOUTH BOSTON, MA—The recently closed Maiden, a gastropub located at 28 W. Broadway in South Boston, had a past life as a mobster hangout for the likes of James "Whitey" Bulger and Stephen "the Rifleman" Flemmi. Triple O's received the nickname as "the Blood House of South Boston" and rightfully so.

Bulger and Flemmi reportedly made decisions at Triple O's as to who they were going to kill or shake down next. Also, there was at least one gang-style murder at the watering hole.

Louis Litif, a cocaine-addicted bookie who ran around with Bulger during his Winter Hill days, angered the Irish mob boss one night in 1982 and was found brutally murdered the following week. "Louis Litif . . . made the worst decision of his life in 1980 when he stopped by Triple O's bar, a notorious mob hangout, to talk with Bulger about some missing bookkeeping money that Bulger suspected Litif was using to buy cocaine," wrote Beverly Ford and Stephanie Schorow in *The Boston Mob Guide*. "Even worse, Litif was refusing to pay Bulger a cut of his trafficking profits and murdered two people without Bulger's permission. It wasn't long before Litif's dead body was wrapped in plastic, hauled out the back door and placed in the trunk of a car, only to be discovered days later at another location."

According to Brian Halloran, a South Boston drug dealer who dropped off Litif at Triple O's that fateful night in May 1982, Bulger stabbed the bookie with an ice pick and then shot Litif to death at the bar. Halloran, who ratted out Bulger to authorities, was murdered outside of Anthony's Pier 4 restaurant overlooking

Boston Harbor along with Michael Donahue, a construction worker with no ties to the gang.

It's believed that Litif was killed upstairs at Triple O's. Apparently, Bulger had an affinity for the second floor. "He liked the ambience of a second-floor room upstairs—its grit and darkness were good for shakedowns, murder plots, and meetings with the nascent IRA," reported the *Boston Phoenix*.

Kevin Weeks, a bouncer at Triple O's and prolific gangster, discussed the murder in his book *Brutal: My Life in Whitey Bulger's Irish Mob*. "Strangely enough, Jimmy told me, 'Louie's last words to me were a lie.' Apparently, Louie had insisted that he'd come by himself and that nobody had driven him over," wrote Weeks. "It was hard to figure out why Louie lied to Jimmy that night. If he'd told Jimmy that someone had driven him, he might have gotten a pass. But it wouldn't have lasted long, since Jimmy had no intention of letting Louie run wild."

The South Boston watering hole had a history of violence long before Bulger set up court at Triple O's. In the 1960s, 28 West Broadway was called Transit Café, headquarters for the Killeen gang known for loan-sharking. It was during this era that the Killeen leader bit off a rival gang member's nose and spat it out before returning inside to celebrate. By the 1980s, the place had reopened as Triple O's, named for the three O'Neil brothers who ran it.

In 2007, the roughneck bar was the scene of a fatal stabbing motivated by a spilled drink.

A twenty-six-year-old Revere man, Adam Rich, died from multiple stab wounds to the chest and stomach after he was attacked at the bar on West Broadway. It was then called the Six House and the perpetrator was identified as Bernard Piscopo.

South Boston has changed dramatically since the senseless slaying in 2007. The neighborhood has gentrified in recent years, and the former Triple O's has been transformed into a series of restaurants, including a sushi joint called Owl Station and most recently the Maiden.

Rachel Hoffman, the founder of Paranormal Xpeditions, investigated the location in 2010 and said the nightlife hot spot is Southie's most haunted.

"In the basement of the Old Triple O's, you can smell gunpowder," Hoffman told *Mass Murders*. "For me, it's the most haunted location I have ever been to. Pots and pans crashed. Nothing moved, but you could hear the crashing noises."

Hoffman, who has been featured on Syfy's *Paranormal Challenge* and the Bio Channel's *My Ghost Story*, said there are skeletal secrets in the building's basement. "There's a drain down there that I believe they used to rinse blood," she said. "I heard what sounded like a body being dragged down the stairs. It made a thud noise, and I caught it on camera."

Hoffman revisited the location when it was Owl Station and said she interacted with the former owner's daughter. "The place had since become a sushi restaurant. I went in and the daughter of the owner exclaimed, 'I knew it was haunted . . . they all call me crazy!' They have renovated since the opening, but there are some things you can never change."

The paranormal investigator and sensitive said she had a psychic vision during the investigation that continues to haunt her.

"The vibration is still with me," she said. "I saw a mummified head in the basement, and it looked to be a young boy with blond curly hair or maybe red. It stays with me."

Hoffman said recent renovations and fresh paint can't wash away Triple O's bloodstained history. "I've never heard accounts to back up what I saw, so I never published that experience," she continued. "But I do know that Bulger paid off parents in Southie to keep their mouths shut."

King Philip

If anyone had the right to seek postmortem justice based on how the Massachusetts Bay colonists handled their native neighbors, it would be the Wampanaogs' sachem Metacom, also known as King Philip.

After he was fatally shot by a "praying Indian" named John Alderman on August 12, 1676, near Mount Hope in Bristol, Rhode Island, his body was cut into quarters and his head was skewered on a pike in the middle of Plymouth's Town Square. As his body was savagely dismembered by a team of rangers led by Captain Benjamin Church, Philip's severed hand was given to his killer as a reward. Alderman reportedly charged a fee for curiosity seekers wanting to sneak a peek of the body part kept in a pail full of rum.

Yes, it's a far cry from the country's first Thanksgiving in 1621 attended by Philip's father, Massasoit, the wise Pokanoket sachem who managed to live peacefully with the early Puritan settlers for forty years.

Metacom initially followed in his father's footsteps. He and his brother, Wamsutta, asked the courts of Plymouth for a proper English name in the spring of 1660. However, the table quickly turned. As soon as Wamsutta assumed the name Alexander, he broke away from his father's diplomacy by joining forces with the Connecticut Colony. He mysteriously died in 1662.

Renamed Philip by the courts in Plymouth, Metacom became the sachem of the Wampanoag confederacy. King Philip, as he was nicknamed by the English, believed that his brother was murdered and led a revolt that would ultimately result in thousands of deaths. He wanted to push the colonists out of New England, but the chief failed miserably. Unfortunately, King Philip's War became a brutal model of how the fledgling country would deal with its native population.

Philip expressed his growing distrust to his colonist friend John Borden of Rhode Island right before the war. "The English who first came to this country were but a handful of people, forlorn, poor, and distressed. My father was then sachem. He relieved their distress in the most kind and hospitable manner," Philip told Borden in 1675. "My elder brother became sachem. They pretended to suspect him of evil designs against them. He was seized and confined and thereby thrown into illness and died."

Philip said the Puritan settlers disarmed his people and then confiscated their lands. He was determined to take a stand to protect his decimated native community. "A small part of the dominion of my ancestors remains," Philip emoted. "I am determined not to live until I have no country."

According to one psychic medium, Philip continues to fight in the afterlife. "He came to me after a table tipping session at an event. He was very upset," said psychic Cheryl Cesarini. "He came through as powerful energy and let me know that he was the chief."

Cesarini said the sachem communicated with her at a historic property in Middleborough, Massachusetts. "He wanted offerings to be done when someone was to come on his land," Cesarini told me. "He also wanted me to burn sage and use a drum to cleanse the house for three days."

The main gist of Cesarini's spirit communication with Philip was about honoring the legacy of his people. "He felt like he was disrespected," Cesarini said. "The chief wants us to know that the land was taken by force, and the spirits of his ancestors have been abused."

KING PHILIP'S HAUNT: BURIAL HILL

PLYMOUTH, MA—Why is "America's Hometown" so haunted? Darcy H. Lee, author of *Ghosts of Plymouth, Massachusetts*, believes the bloodstained events that unfolded in the early seventeenth century have left a psychic imprint on the land surrounding Burial Hill in Plymouth's Town Square.

"When the Pilgrims landed in 1620, there were more than 100 on board and only 50 survived," Lee told me. "One of the most haunted places is Town Square, which is near the place where the Pilgrims had their first settlement. Just prior to the Pilgrims' landing, there was a plague that decimated the Native Americans that lived there. The desperation and fear of the Native Americans who lived and died there is embedded into the ground."

Based purely on its historical legacy and the harsh conditions that nearly annihilated America's earliest settlers in 1620, Plymouth is one of New England's most haunted cities. Burial Hill, the town's oldest cemetery, is nestled next to First Parish in Plymouth and located across the street from the Church of the Pilgrimage and the 1749 Court House.

The chaos from four centuries ago still lingers in Plymouth's Town Square. It's almost as if the death and destruction have psychically imprinted on the location.

Lee believes there's a Native American spirit guarding Burial Hill near the Cushman Monument. "Legend has it that there is a spot on Burial Hill on top of the staircase by a huge tree," Lee wrote in *Ghosts of Plymouth, Massachusetts*. "The tree has a peculiar feature. It has roots that look like hands. Some say a Native American guardian sits and watches over people at that tree. If a visitor to Burial Hill does anything unacceptable or inappropriate, the guardian spirit will let them know in a terrifying fashion."

Luckily, the Native American sentinel spirit likes me. However, I had a not-so-friendly encounter in early 2018 with a spirit known as "Crazy Mary." She paces back and forth near the cemetery's stairs facing Town Square. When I approached Burial Hill, she lunged at me, and I quickly ran down the stairs and back to my room at the John Carver Inn. "She likes to scare people," said Geoffrey Campbell when I told him about my face-to-face encounter with the aggressive female spirit. "She's very sad because people misunderstand her," he told me. "She does scare people off depending on their sensitivities. I had one woman on my tour who walked up the stairs and came running back down the hill. She said that something came after her."

Mary isn't necessarily mentally ill, but she seems to get a kick out of chasing clairvoyants out of the burial ground.

Campbell, a veteran guide and operator of the Plymouth Night Tour, led me through the extremely haunted cemetery, which is home to several ghosts including Scary Mary, a Native American sentinel spirit, a Victorian-era couple and possibly a cryptid known as a Pukwudgie.

Never heard of this mythical creature associated with Plymouth's Wampanoag tribe? It's a little trickster that boasts large ears, fingers, and nose. Based on reports, including a mention in Henry Wadsworth Longfellow's epic poem "The Song of Hiawatha," the human-shaped gremlin has smooth, gray skin.

Campbell told me that he's seen Burial Hill's Pukwudgies in action. "I was giving a tour a few years ago, and we saw three of them dancing around," Campbell insisted. "People were trying to take pictures, but it didn't pick up." One tour guide, Vicki Noel Harrington, was in a picture taken outside of the John Carver Inn next to Burial Hill. According to people who have seen the photo, the image looks like a demon peeking over her shoulder.

Campbell believes the "demon" seen in the picture with Harrington is actually a Pukwudgie. "They tend to hide by the mass grave for the soldiers from the brigantine *General Arnold*," he said, pointing to an area in the back next to a copse of trees. "We've had several sightings from the path leading to the monument."

Of course, the story about the ill-fated mariners of the *General Arnold* is legendary in Plymouth. During a Christmas Eve blizzard in 1778, seventy-two men literally froze to death after the vessel and its crew, led by Captain James Magee, were stranded on a sandbar in Plymouth Harbor.

"Captain Magee told them to put rum in their shoes to ward off frostbite, but many drank it instead, dying quickly thereafter, their bodies frozen where they sat or stood," wrote Emily Wilcox in *Wicked Local Plymouth* in 2007. "Seamen huddled together against the blinding snow, whistling winds and crashing waves. Some tried to wrap the heavy, canvas sail around themselves to no avail. They shrieked prayers to God and screamed for help from their fellow man. But the *General Arnold* was beyond help."

Campbell said that when the men were retrieved in Plymouth Harbor, many of them were frozen in grotesque shapes, some clutching each other in a horrific death grip while others were stacked on top of each other to block the treacherous nor'easter storm.

The bodies of more than seventy frozen soldiers were kept in the 1749 Court House before being buried in a mass grave located in the rear of the cemetery. "The courthouse basically served as a temporary morgue," Campbell said. "I've heard that the courthouse has a residual haunting associated with the tragedy." At the 1749 Court House in Town Square, people have heard phantom footsteps and what sounded like ice melting.

According to several reports, the captain of the brigantine, James Magee, has been spotted in the cemetery, paying postmortem respect to his fallen crew. Darcy H. Lee, author of *Ghosts of Plymouth, Massachusetts*, confirmed the rumors. "We do know that Captain James McGee visited their gravesite, and his is a residual haunting in Burial Hill as well," she told me. "It's that imprint of what they were doing in life that remains."

Like Lee, Campbell believes that the spirits haunting Burial Hill are just visiting. "When people see apparitions specifically in this cemetery, they are not usually people who were buried here," Campbell confirmed. "I find that the apparitions are usually here to visit someone buried in the cemetery. I also believe there's a portal in Burial Hill, and spirits are able to come through, visit their loved ones, and then return to where they came from."

Lee said that one haunting associated with Burial Hill involves a Victorian-era couple who visited the gravestone of their two-year-old daughter, Ida Elizabeth Spear. "Their grief and sadness remain as a residual haunting in Burial Hill. People spot them walking up and down the pathways of the cemetery."

Of course, this theory applies to a recent tragedy that mysteriously happened on September 8, 2010. Michael "Wolf" Pasakarnis, a Plymouth-based poet and artist, was freakishly struck by lightning on his way home from Blue Blinds Bakery on North Street. Many believe that the twenty-nine-year-old man, known for his piercing eyes and heart of gold, predicted his freakish and untimely death, which was posthumously revealed in his cryptic drawings and writings. In fact, Pasakarnis wrote a poem claiming that "the time has come to allow the light of nature to free my soul" a few days before he passed.

Throughout the Burial Hill tour, Campbell kept finding offerings like a turkey feather and a heart-shaped rock. "This is from my friend Wolf," Campbell confirmed, pointing out that the Jack Skellington hat he was wearing was an homage to Pasakarnis. Apparently, *A Nightmare Before Christmas* was Wolf's favorite movie, and Campbell led me to the tree where the young man was found dead from electrocution in 2010. There were markings alluding to Wolf's life and love for *Nightmare*, including a "Pumpkin King" smile, etched into the tree. "They originally thought Wolf fell from the tree," Campbell said, recounting Wolf's prophetic last day. "He was with friends at the bakery and then dropped off a heart-shaped rock at the Laughing Moon boutique before heading up to Court Street and finally to Burial Hill."

According to an article by Emily Clark in the November 21, 2010, edition of *Wicked Local*, Wolf left an indelible impact on Plymouth's tight-knit community. "He was standing next to a beech tree when the bolt hit him, exploding his iPod and exiting out the heel of boots his father had just bought him, leaving a jagged hole behind," Clark wrote. "His death stunned a community of friends and downtown regulars who had come to rely on his compassion, his daily walks through town, and that mysterious otherworldliness that made so many believe in magic and in things happening for a reason."

When Campbell showed me a picture of Wolf, I gasped. He looked so familiar. In fact, I had recurring dreams of what I thought was a young, Native American man encouraging me to come to Plymouth. It was Wolf.

When I said that I had connected with Wolf's spirit in my dreams, Campbell wasn't surprised. It seemed that the young man had connected with other mediums in the past. One clairvoyant, Suzanne Giesemann, wrote an entire book called *Wolf's Message* in 2014 about her psychic interactions with his spirit.

As Campbell and I were talking, the mystery surrounding this mysterious man continued. His mother, Beth, was visiting Burial

Hill from out of town and overheard our discussion. She walked up and started sharing stories about her son. It was a few days before the anniversary of his death, so she was in town to pay respect and commemorate her son.

"It's almost as if he lived between two worlds," Pasakarnis told me. "When he left the bakery, he told his friends that he 'had to go,' as if he knew he had to be here at that time. Even the storm was strange. It came out of nowhere, and there was only one random lightning strike."

When I mentioned that I wanted to dedicate a convention that I produced called the Plymouth ParaCon to her son, she said that he would "get a kick out of it," implying that his spirit is still around. Based on the randomness of meeting his mother in Burial Hill, the feathers and heart-shaped rocks dotting our journey, and the recurring dreams, I believe his spirit was around us that day.

Campbell, who regularly eulogizes Wolf on his tours, promised to place two roses at Wolf's tree on the anniversary of his death. He also handed Pasakarnis a feather that he found next to the Cushman Monument. "Here's a gift from Wolf," he said. The mother's eyes started to well up with emotion. "He would leave something like this," Pasakarnis said with a smile. "He's always letting us know that he's still here in spirit."

Orleans Waterfront Inn

After my first overnight at the allegedly haunted Orleans Waterfront Inn on July Fourth weekend in Cape Cod a few years ago, the fireworks oddly happened *inside* this historic, nineteenth-century structure. As far as my sensitivity to the paranormal, my so-called "ghostdar" was off the hook as soon as I walked into this seasonal restaurant and inn. I somehow chose the haunted spot, which is Room 5. Unbeknownst to me at the time, my bed for the night made a cameo on an episode of Syfy's *Ghost Hunters.*

"Built in 1875, the inn was initially a hardware store and was then renovated into a speakeasy run by the Irish mob, as well as a bordello," reported *MassLive* in a recap of the 2010 TAPS investigation. "There was a murder on the premises. One of the prostitutes was found dead outside of the inn. Various other apparitions were reported, including two of the workers who committed suicide, both by hanging, on the premises and a naked woman dancing in the lobby."

I purposely don't do research before going to a supposedly haunted location. When I booked the hotel, I liked the room's name, which is simply "1875," a hat tip to the year it was built. Of course, I chose the suite where guests check in but refuse to check out. Yes, according to reports, two women, who were "not right," once refused to leave the room on their own accord. Employees at the inn claimed they would hear what sounded like an animal growling and possibly a foreign language that sounded like German when one woman barricaded herself inside the second-floor locale.

"We are also told about the history of Room 5 where not one but two women checked in for a weekend and then stayed for about five months, only being removed forcefully from the rooms, one by family, one by the police," reported *MassLive*.

Owner Ed Maas, who purchased the haunted hotel in 1996, wrote about the room in his book *Ghost of the Orleans Inn*. He believes the room's haunting relates to the reported suicide of a German visitor in the inn's downstairs bathroom.

"Although the cause of death may have been determined, it is unclear of the manner. If it was by a knife, was the owner of it perhaps escorted away from the scene? There is little information about the death, and little is ever spoken of it," Maas wrote. "The room above the restroom is particularly interesting. Guests check in for a short stay and seem unwilling to leave. One particular guest exhibited multiple personalities as a German SS soldier. To hear the German's cursing coming from the elderly female was frightening. It seemed as if German interrogations were going on behind closed doors."

Within the first hour of my stay, I chatted with the owner's daughter, Meaghan, who gave me a brief walk-through of the location, which has been featured in various paranormal books. In the lobby, a "hidden room" once housed bootlegged liquor and provided cover for various other underworld activities during its

Irish mobster-era heyday. Meaghan told me about the history of my room and recounted the story of how two previous guests had refused to leave. "It's definitely a room with a strange history," she joked, struggling to unlock the door. "You should definitely visit the cupola upstairs before it gets dark."

Within the first hour, I went to the top floor and read a letter to "Hannah," the resident spirit of the 1875 inn. I carried an Ovilus with me as I walked through the hotel's belvedere and then creeped up into the cupola. The air in the small room overlooking Orleans's Town Cove felt psychically charged, as if something horrible had happened there. With the Ovilus, I picked up "with" when I asked if the spirit was with us. It also said "Jones" and "devil" when I asked who had murdered the inn's resident ghost.

I had an intense reaction in the cupola, as if the spirit in the room wanted to communicate with me. It was a male energy, and the spirit box kept spitting out words like "rubber" and "sex." In fact, the novelty investigation tool spewed out words so fast, I had to turn it off. The spirit seemed sexually charged and somewhat misogynistic. I didn't know it at the time, but the cupola is where the bartender, Fred, had hanged himself in the 1950s.

The cupola is also where Steve Gonsalves from *Ghost Hunters* picked up an EVP that sounded like "Let me out." However, Gonsalves believed it said "Get me down."

When Mark Jasper wrote about the Orleans Waterfront Inn in *Haunted Cape Cod*, he appropriately named the chapter on the inn "Gangsters & Ghosts."

"The house was originally built in 1875 by Aaron Snow II for his wife and seven children," wrote Jasper. "He was a direct descendant of Constance Hopkins, who was the first person to spot Cape Cod from the *Mayflower* as it sailed near Eastham in 1620. Hannah and Fred are thought to be the two ghosts responsible for some of the bizarre incidents that have transpired in the inn over the years. Unsure of the identities of the murdered prostitutes, the Maases named the female ghost Hannah. Fred, you recall, was the bartender who hanged himself in the cupola. Hannah apparently loves to play with doors."

She also apparently loves to play with paranormal researchers. My overnight stay in this extremely haunted hotel was terrifyingly memorable. As I was sitting on the bed and reaching for my computer, I felt something rub up against my leg. I told my friend about the bizarre sensation. It turns out the inn has a history of "ghost cats," specifically in the neighboring Room 4.

I also captured an EVP outside of the inn that still haunts me. I was sitting on a bench near the 300-year-old Jonathan Young windmill, and I had what I can only describe as a psychic moment in which I relived what I believe to be the murder of the young woman who still lingers in the inn. Based on my vision, she was in love with one of her suitors, and he shot her because she knew too much. I have no idea what the vision means, except that she was completely not expecting to be shot outside of the structure known as "Aaron's Folly" by a man she was courting.

During the EVP session, I asked the spirit if she was murdered. I picked up what sounded like a whispering female—a whispering that got progressively louder as the recording continued. When I asked her to tell me her name, I clearly picked up what sounded like either "Anna" or "Hannah." I was in shock. I quickly packed up my things and went inside. I thought about leaving the haunted Orleans inn after that eerie EVP session. However, I was scheduled to interview the owner the following morning.

One of the first things Ed Maas heard from the locals after he purchased the historic Orleans Waterfront Inn in 1996 was that the property was notoriously haunted and that it would be in his best interest not to upset the ghosts.

When asked if he knew the Orleans inn was haunted before he purchased it, Maas shook his head. "I had no idea," he told me. "I had driven by the inn for twenty-five years and never came inside. It was slated to be knocked down, and I wasn't told by the Realtor. After we purchased it, I then found out that the inn was written about in the *Cape Cod Times*, and I called the Realtor and asked them about it, and I quickly learned the inn was rumored to be haunted. We then made ourselves comfortable with the ghosts."

Maas initially shrugged off the spirited stories until he had a face-to-face encounter with the female apparition of a ghost he now calls Hannah. "When we bought the inn, I would stay here around the clock. At midnight, I would lie on the couch to get some sleep. In the middle of the night, I saw what I thought was one of the guests come downstairs stark naked. I said 'Hello,' and she said 'Hello' back. I didn't think much of it until a woman stopped her car outside of the inn a few days later after seeing a naked woman dancing in the fifth-floor belvedere. That's when I put two and two together."

The owner said he had his first encounter with Hannah in 2000. When I asked him if he'd had any experiences with the ghosts outside the property, he quickly told me that that's where she'd been killed.

"Hannah was murdered outside," he explained. "We believe she lived in Room 5, but most of the sightings have been in Room 4. In fact, we just had a group record an EVP session with Hannah, and they asked her if she was happy, and she said she was. During the Roaring Twenties, this was a house of ill-repute. We believe the spirit is the woman who was murdered here in the 1920s."

Maas, the father of eight children, said his family is at peace with the inn's resident spirits. "We don't tell the guests about the ghosts before they check in," he continued. "Some people know about it, and some come here specifically for the hauntings. It's not something that we really promote. My wife says, 'Don't upset the ghosts.' We look at it as Hannah's inn. It's her home, and we take care of it for her."

HANNAH'S HAUNT: ORLEANS WATERFRONT INN

CAPE COD, MA—Want to see if a "room with a boo" is truly haunted? Work the graveyard shift at an allegedly haunted hotel.

For the past few years, I signed on as a night auditor at several boo-tique inns, including the Hotel 140 in Boston's Back Bay neighborhood. Right above the front desk is the Lyric Stage Company theater. Multiple times in the wee hours of the night, I encountered a female spirit who'd mysteriously try to lead me upstairs. I'm not sure what her deal was, but she was desperately trying to communicate with me.

One Monday night in May 2017 when I was working the overnight shift at Hotel 140, I met Lyric Stage Company of

Boston's associate production manager, Stephanie Hettrick. We started chatting, and within the first few minutes, she revealed to me that my hunch was true: the former YWCA turned hotel is in fact haunted. "We call her Alice," Hettrick said, speaking quietly so her friend couldn't hear her talking about the building's resident ghost. "She doesn't like me, but she likes my boss. He was away for a week and it caused all sorts of problems. Things would mysteriously move. Lights would turn on and off. We blamed it on Alice."

When I asked her if she knew anything about Alice's backstory, Hettrick said she strongly believed the female spirit was in her early to late twenties. I asked her how she knew so many details about the ghostly woman, and the production manager smiled. "Because I've seen her," she said, pointing to the second-floor mezzanine level of the hotel and the side-stairs area Alice was known to frequent. "She's wearing white, and sometimes when I'm here late at night in the theater, I will see her out of the corner of my eye."

Hettrick's friend, who was in the ladies' room behind Hotel 140's front desk, ran out in a tizzy. "Are you talking about ghosts? If you are, then I'm going to leave now." Her friend was joking, but you could see she was obviously creeped out by the hotel's resident spirit.

Of course, the ghost story from Hotel 140 was purely anecdotal. I wanted proof, so I reached out to the owner of what I believed was the most haunted bed and breakfast in New England: Orleans Waterfront Inn located on Old Country Road in Cape Cod.

As someone who has worked the paranormal night shift at various hotels, I oddly hadn't participated in a formal investigation at one of these overnight haunts until the owner of the inn, Ed Maas, agreed to host my group in 2017.

I normally work by myself or with a small team when I communicate with the spirits featured in my books. However, during that memorable night, I handpicked a crew of experienced investigators including Russ Stiver and his partner, Nicole Hellested, coupled with a few newbies including my skeptic friend Andrew Warburton and former-wrestler-turned-empath Jeremy Cotter and his wife, Jean.

I jokingly called our group "Team Cellar Dwellers," or TCD, because this particular combination of people always ended up investigating in the basement of an allegedly haunted location.

For the September 30, 2017, investigation, we had the entire inn to ourselves, which served us well because we didn't have issues with noise contamination. When we arrived at the location, I was more focused on solving the crime involving Hannah, the female spirit who was supposedly murdered outside of the inn. I wanted to give her a voice; however, the ghosts led us down a completely different path.

Stiver, a fellow sensitive and investigator, said he was chased up the stairs by a shadow figure near the historic structure's cupola area within the first ten minutes. This location was also said to be the site of a suicide involving a former bartender, who supposedly hanged himself. Jeremy Cotter started picking up on a German spirit, and our focus quickly changed.

For the National Ghost Hunting Day event, we used equipment that I normally don't use, including the EchoVox, an iPhone app used for spirit communication. I also brought my Sherlock

Holmes tarot deck that surprisingly helped us piece together a cohesive story as the evening progressed. I also used old-school tools on my investigations including dowsing rods, pendulums, digital recorders, and tarot cards. Stiver used more high-tech tools like a spirit box.

My Sherlock Holmes tarot cards were incredibly accurate as was the EchoVox during the investigation.

At the time, I had little knowledge of the inn's past involving an elderly woman who checked into Room 5 and then refused to leave. According to Maas, he noticed that she started to speak in a language that sounded German and, based on his retelling of the story to me, her voice sounded male.

In addition to the potentially possessed guest, the inn had a past life as a bordello. Our first encounter in Room 4 involved a female spirit trying to communicate but who wasn't allowed to speak by an overbearing male energy in the room. Most of the people on the investigation didn't know that the Orleans Waterfront Inn was formerly a house of ill-repute. Somehow, most of the sensitives in the group picked up on the illicit activities that happened there, including possible ties to the mob.

During the investigation, the German spirit led us to the basement. It was in the hotel's lower level that we set up our equipment at the spot where Paul, the inn's former cook, supposedly committed suicide. At the spot where the cook's body was found, we kept picking up the names "Paul and Ed."

We also got multiple threats, like "kill" and "leave," over the EchoVox and spirit box. When Stiver asked who was in the room, the audio equipment said "Sam," and my skeptic friend, Andrew

Warburton, spotted a shadow figure dart by our group in the lower level. The words on the EchoVox got progressively angry as the investigation continued, and the entity didn't like when my tarot cards picked up on a possible homicide happening in the basement, which came through our ghost hunting equipment.

What was the outcome of the investigation? I had a long conversation with the current owner of the Orleans Waterfront Inn, and I asked him about some of the evidence we uncovered the night before. I couldn't figure out why the name "Ed" came up over and over. In fact, one response was "Talk to Ed."

It turns out that the former owner of the inn shared Maas's first name and initials. Ed Martin, the previous proprietor, recently passed, and he was the owner when Paul, the cook, was found hanging in the basement. The death was ruled a suicide but, like the other questionable deaths in the building, it seemed sketchy.

I asked Maas about the German connections. I was shocked to learn that the former owner was German, so all of the information from the evening's investigation started to make sense. My intuition suggested that there were possible ties to a German submarine that attacked Orleans during World War I on July 21, 1918. Also, there was an unreported "suicide" that happened at the inn during the early 1900s involving a German man found in what is now the downstairs bathroom.

Did we connect with the infamous Hannah during our investigation at Orleans Waterfront Inn? Nope. However, we did stumble upon an unexpected subplot that suggests a potential cover-up. Next time, I'll bring a German translator.

Crime Q&A:
Christopher Balzano

*I've discovered that Native American or even witch stories
are often used to cover up racial tensions. It's as if history hasn't
allowed us to admit what we did to these
marginalized groups of people.*
— *Christopher Balzano,* Dark Woods

For Christopher Balzano, author of *Dark Woods* and host of the *Tripping on Legends* podcast, there's no place like home. When asked what he missed most about New England after his move from

Massachusetts to Florida, he took a deep breath. "The question makes me too depressed to even answer," he said with a laugh.

Truthfully, it's a tough one, especially for the noted folklorist who became immersed in the legends associated with his extraordinarily weird home state. "There's just so much," he said, referring specifically to the outrageous lore that has emerged from the Freetown State Forest located on the edge of what is called the Bridgewater Triangle. "Whether it's Pukwudgies or the cult issue or why odd things find their way there, you can only go so far before you eventually slam against a wall or a speed bump of not knowing."

In the interview, Balzano talked about the unexplained mysteries that he explored growing up in Massachusetts and the ultimate question he asked himself while writing *Dark Woods*: Can the same energy that seems to feed paranormal activity also attract other things like entities, cryptids, and crimes? "In researching the area and its history," he said, "I was constantly surprised at how many leads ended in 'I don't know' or a shrug."

Q: In hindsight, what are your thoughts about the Fall River Cult Murders?

A: It's a difficult case that in many ways has less to do with the oddness of the area and more to do with the tone and atmosphere of the town. The Bridgewater Triangle may have made for an excellent backdrop for the crimes and the characters and had a subtle influence over the people involved, but ultimately Carl Drew and Robin Murphy were really just into some odd things that were popular in the area at the time and practiced in some shape or form by a lot of the people in the scene. They were just better at manipulating the people around them.

Q: Do you think murders leave a psychic imprint or an "aura of disaster" at a location?

A: Any highly emotional event where there's a sudden or powerful release of psychic energy is going to leave an impression that may then be replayed or even trapped. The real question is whether that imprint attracts other things and invites them in, which is the underlying theme of *Dark Woods*. If you leave the science alone, and at some point you need to, there's enough anecdotal evidence that bad things, or even different kinds of paranormal events, occur in the same place over and over.

Q: There are so many legends associated with the Freetown State Forest. Do you think they are based on actual true stories?

A: All legends are based on some degree of truth, so the easy answer is "yes." People had experiences, which are a combination of potential supernatural and paranormal events and a true misunderstanding of the natural world, especially with so much untamed parts of the forest. The only way to process this information is through previous knowledge, much of which is based on a familiarity with folklore and even old ghost stories.

Q: Do you think Freetown State Forest is cursed? If so, why?

A: Cursed is a loaded word. There's a cloud of darkness over the area, which draws in and then draws from. A curse implies someone started this, and through all of my years of trying to discover a reason, all I keep finding is that what was once a cause always tends to become the effect of something before it. Simply, there's no cause. Cursed, of course, is a nice, comfortable word to help us understand.

Q: There are so many hauntings associated with the Freetown State Forest. Any stand out to you?
A: The Assonet Ledge is one of the most active locations. But the experiences of the individuals I've talked to in the homes across town and the area as a whole stand out the most. Residential locations are just like any other location, but there are so many families who've had odd experiences with no obvious backstory who seem to suffer the most from the Bridgewater Triangle effect.

Q: Any proof that the area was the site of a Native American massacre at the hands of the Puritans?
A: I haven't found any evidence of that in Freetown. There was a mention in a book implying that there was a massacre of slaves in the forest, but I haven't been able to find this information myself. I've tracked legends here in Florida over the last few years, and I've discovered that Native American or even witch stories are often used to cover up racial tensions. It's as if history hasn't allowed us to admit what we did to these marginalized groups of people.

Crime Scenes:
Hometown Hauntings

*Those that have seen the ghost say that she resembles
a woman from the 1920s or a flapper.*

—*Ian Judge, Somerville Theatre*

If I had to handpick two cities that should have been featured in *Mass Murders*, they would be Somerville and Malden. Of course, I'm biased. I've lived in Somerville for years, and I'm the former coordinator of a citizen journalism project produced by Malden Access TV.

When it comes to the most haunted crime scenes in the state, there's no place like home.

I had my first spirited encounter as an adult while living in Somerville's Ball Square in the early 1990s. I recall seeing an apparition of a young girl who would play hide-and-seek in the hallway. She was a mischievous poltergeist, and I remember hearing phantom footsteps leading to our second-floor apartment.

Author Sam Baltrusis is based in Somerville, Massachusetts.
PHOTO BY FRANK C. GRACE

Since returning to Somerville in 2007, I've spent years investigating alleged accounts of paranormal activity at sites all over New England. I've collected a slew of reports from these supposedly haunted locales, and the mission was to give readers a contemporary take on the bevy of site-specific legends. *Mass Murders* is a cautionary tale written with a paranormal lens. This book is about the people—the villains and the victims—who left an indelible, psychic imprint at these allegedly haunted locations scattered throughout Massachusetts.

While researching my third book, *Ghosts of Salem: Haunts of the Witch City*, in 2013, I managed a pop-up Spirit Halloween store in what would become my new neighborhood in Somerville's Assembly Square. The seasonal shop was located in an abandoned Circuit City building and had a history of squatters and vandals before it became a Halloween store. During my initial interview, a manager from another region asked me about my books. I told her.

She looked at me and sheepishly said: "You know this place is haunted, right?" I laughed. Why would a former Circuit City have paranormal activity? She told me that several employees had heard inexplicable phantom footsteps in the back storage area near the loading dock. Oddly, some of the store's animatronics would mysteriously turn on and off. Shadow figures were seen through the glass. She also heard what sounded like residual gunshots in the storage area.

The idea of a haunted Halloween store seemed a bit too good to be true. However, she was right. I regularly heard mysterious footsteps in the back area. I also experienced recurring poltergeist activity that involved one of our props, a creepy plastic rat.

The ghosts of Spirit Halloween were trying to tell me something, and it involved a rat or, in 1950s-era speak, a snitch. Before closing the store, I would check to see if all our decor was shelved appropriately. I especially kept an eye on our creepy-crawly section, which included spooky animals and a larger-than-life plastic rodent.

I also had to set the alarm so there was no way anybody could have been playing a practical joke. The following morning, without fail, I would open and find a rat strategically placed somewhere in the store. It became a daily ritual of sorts that I jokingly called "find the rat."

In 2015, I returned to Somerville's haunted Halloween store, and the residual energy still lingered there. Why return? I recently moved into the new Assembly Square apartment complex facing the Mystic River, and I decided to make a comeback as Spirit Halloween's store manager. It's easy access.

I talked with people who worked in the building when it was a Circuit City, and one woman claimed that she regularly heard phantom footsteps. "Yeah, I always thought this place was haunted," she said. "I'm not surprised it's a Halloween store. I bet the ghosts are having fun here."

One Spirit Halloween employee, Christine Broderick, claimed she had a close encounter with the ghost in the loading dock area. "I was in the warehouse breaking up boxes, and my hair got pulled hard and I saw a man standing a few feet away. He was probably about five feet and eleven inches and had light brown, blondish hair," Broderick recalled. "I screamed. He disappeared. I'm starting to get freaked out because I don't know why he doesn't like me?"

Assembly Square got its name from the Ford Motor Company's assembly plant built there in 1926. It was also a hub for the Boston and Maine Railroad. The assembly plant closed in 1958, and the initial theory was that the ghosts were somehow tied to the plant.

Somerville also has a history of modern-era gangsters, so "the rat" may literally be mob related. Of course, the notorious James "Whitey" Bulger made headlines for years until he was

Spot the rat? A pop-up Spirit Halloween store in Somerville's Assembly Square is allegedly haunted by a disgruntled spirit.
PHOTO BY SAM BALTRUSIS

murdered in West Virginia's United States Penitentiary, Hazelton, on October 29, 2018. Bulger earned his Winter Hill Gang moniker from his former hangout in the city's Winter Hill neighborhood, which is right next to Assembly Square. Truthfully, Bulger did most of his seedy, underworld activity in South Boston, but he definitely spent time in what is now my neighborhood in Somerville.

I've been told by multiple people that a hush-hush crime happened in the building. According to local lore, a criminal hid in the building and was found by the police. "My dad said that a guy escaped from prison and was found in the loading dock area," said one of my employees, Brittany Dean. "Cops found him there and shot him."

While the story is unsubstantiated, it would explain some of the activity in the loading dock area, including the phantom steps and inexplicable gunshot sounds. It's as if the murder of the man is a residual haunting or a videotaped replay of tragic, past events.

However, things also have been mysteriously moved throughout the location. Based on my experience, I would categorize the haunting as a "stay behind," a type of spirit that doesn't know he's dead due to the circumstances of his death.

The late Dr. Hans Holzer, in an interview in 2005, explained the phenomenon. " 'Stay behinds' are relatively common," he said. "Somebody dies, and then they're really surprised that all of a sudden they're not dead. They're alive like they were. They don't understand it because they weren't prepared for it. So they go back to what they knew most—their chair, their room, and they just sit there. Next, they want to let people know that they're still 'alive.' So they'll do little things like moving things, appear to relatives, pushing objects, poltergeist phenomena, and so on."

I've had several encounters with "stay behinds" in Somerville. The first was a female spirit I jokingly called "Scissor Sister."

Before moving into Assembly Row, I fled my room with a "boo!" in Somerville's Davis Square. The house's resident ghost, a playful older female poltergeist with an affinity for scissors, did various things in the house to make her presence known. According to a psychic who visited the two-floor Gothic-decorated haunt, she was a seamstress during the Depression era. While I was writing my first book, *Ghosts of Boston*, an unseen force opened doors that were firmly shut, and lights mysteriously turned on and off without provocation. One night, I spotted a full-bodied apparition of a gray-haired female figure wearing an old-school white nightgown and donning fuzzy slippers dart across the first floor while I stood, in shock, at the top of the stairs.

The ghostly incidents escalated after the initial encounter. While I was preparing for the launch party for my first book at Boston's Old South Meeting House, the scissors sitting on the front-room table mysteriously started to spin, and one night, during an interview on *Paranormal Insider Radio*, I heard a loud knock on my bedroom door. I quickly opened it, but no one was there. Oddly, the phantom knocking continued throughout the phone interview. I wasn't afraid.

The gig was up. I decided to move.

Master psychic Denise Fix picked up on the spirit of the seamstress during our second interview. "She's not trying to scare you. She wants your attention," Fix said, sitting at a table that, oddly, was a repurposed Singer sewing machine. "She sewed for many people and felt quite tortured a lot of the time. She was celebrated by you, and she thanks you for that. She was released from whatever bound her there," Fix continued. "And it wasn't a good thing to be bound there."

Two weeks later, I moved out. My last night in the house was memorable. My roommate's exotic parrot escaped from its cage and perched on the oven's open flame. The bird was quickly engulfed in flames but didn't catch fire. While carrying boxes down the stairs, I slipped. I felt something hold me back as I watched the box fall down the stairs. Glass shattered. It could have been me. I fled the haunted house on Hall Avenue and haven't looked back.

I'm often asked what is the most haunted hot spot in my home city? I say without hesitation that it's the Somerville Theatre in Davis Square.

If the ominous red-eyed owls peering from the historic theater's marquee and peeking out from the labyrinthine hallways aren't enough to give you the chills, then its ghost lore involving a 1920s-era flapper will have your hair standing on end.

Built in 1914 by the Boston-based firm Funk & Wilcox, the Somerville Theatre was originally designed for stage shows, opera, vaudeville, and, eventually, motion pictures. Before the Depression, the building boasted a basement café, bowling alley, billiards hall, and the Hobbs Crystal Ballroom, a large dance space on the second floor that could easily host up to 700 fox-trotting partygoers. During its vaudeville heyday in 1915, the stage had its own stock company, the Somerville Theatre Players, and welcomed future icons like Tallulah Bankhead, Francis X. Bushman, and Ray Bolger, who played the Scarecrow in MGM's *The Wizard of Oz.* Kay Corbett, who was part of the vaudeville-era sister act known as the Corbett Revue, also regularly appeared.

A ghostly flapper is said to inhabit rows J and K in the main theater's orchestra-right section of the Somerville Theatre in Davis Square. PHOTO BY JASON BAKER

Apparently, the schedule was grueling for the Somerville Players. They launched a new play each week and performed twice a day. "We rehearse every morning from nine till twelve and then lunch, then a matinee every day, then dinner, then evening performances," wrote

Bankhead in a letter to her grandfather dated 1919. "I'm nearly dead now and I have only been here a week."

For its grand opening on May 11, 1914, the 1,000-plus-seat auditorium showcased a bevy of live acts, including the Stewart Sisters, a comedy skit from the Fuller-Rose company called "A King for a Day," singing by the Adairs, and a two-reel film presentation of *The Inventor's Wife*. Joseph Hobbs, who leased and eventually sold the theater to Arthur F. Viano in 1926, hired an up-and-comer and future film director Busby Berkeley, who went on to produce a slew of stylish musicals including *42nd Street*. The entertainment complex was a featured stop for seventeen years until the Depression's economic tumult forced it to become a movies-only establishment in 1932.

It's around this time that a ghost from its vaudeville past returned to claim her favorite seat in the main auditorium. "The story which has been told to me by two different unrelated sources is that there's an apparition around rows J and K in the orchestra-right section of the main theater here, which was built for movies and vaudeville in 1914," said Ian Judge, the director of operations at the Somerville Theatre. "Some have seen her, and others have just seen the chair cushions in that section move. Those that have seen the ghost say that she resembles a woman from the 1920s or a flapper."

Judge, who eventually got validation about the haunting from a former office manager and the executive director of the Boston SciFi Film Festival, Garen Daly, said he had a close encounter with the flapper ghost when he first started his job years ago. "While I have never seen an apparition, I did see the seats move in a hard-to-explain way," Judge explained. "I was doing some cleaning and renovation work overnight in the balcony. I was all alone, not another person in the building. As I was cleaning, I heard the sound of the seat cushions moving, as if someone were bouncing them up and down . . . they fold up, as theater seats often do. I rushed to the edge of the balcony and looked down and saw two of the seat cushions moving up and down, and they came to a stop as I watched. There was nobody else there, and nobody went out any of the exit doors."

The director of operations said he hadn't heard any stories about the flapper ghost until years after his close encounter. "I've never experienced anything since then, even though I've been alone here hundreds of times," Judge said. "I guess perhaps it was just the ghost welcoming me to my new job."

So, why haunted theaters? Holly Nadler, author of *Ghosts of Boston Town*, believes it's the romantic aesthetic. "All old and beautiful theaters look haunted, with their shadowy corridors, flickering lanterns, vaulted ceilings and Gothic ornaments," she wrote. "They also sound haunted, from the creaking of the woodwork, the rustling of old pipes, the sighs of air currents trapped inside thick stone walls. And indeed, there are some who contend that all old and beautiful theaters really are haunted."

Judge, among the believers, said he's still spooked. However, he has no clue who or what haunts the Somerville Theatre. "I don't know," he said when asked about the ghost's identity. "While nobody has ever died here that we know of, perhaps those were her favorite seats? Back in the days when we had a stock theater company performing on stage around the movie season, people likely had reserved or favorite seats. Maybe she was a matinee-idol fan?"

One theory involves a former ticket seller, a die-hard fan of the Somerville Theatre and regular attendee of the stock theater company until she lost her vision. Sallie B. Irish, twenty-eight years old, committed suicide by jumping out of a fourth-story window in the Back Bay on May 10, 1923. "She had a nervous breakdown, involving trouble with her eyes, since which time she had worked [at the Somerville Theatre] only occasionally," reported the *Boston Daily Globe.* Irish apparently loved the theater and became hysterical when she started having vision problems. She was found dead on Massachusetts Avenue after jumping from her bedroom window. "Miss Irish was very popular about the Somerville Theatre and with its patrons, having worked there eight years," the *Globe* continued.

Perhaps Irish has made a postmortem return to her favorite seats in the main theater? Yes, all the world's a stage . . . and all the lingering spirits merely players.

Behind the Somerville Theatre is the revamped Sacco's Bowl Haven, a candlepin bowling alley, which was renovated by the crew from the Flatbread Company. Back in 2009, crews from the *Ghost Hunters* television show arrived to investigate a few strange occurrences—an inexplicable dark shadow, the sound of childlike laughter from the area behind the candlepin alleys, and even reports of the ghost of a former worker, Charlie, who was supposedly lingering in the maintenance room.

Such happenings seemed fitting for a space that exuded so much history. Originally opened in 1939, Sacco's remained a total throwback to the 1950s until 2010, when renovations added a wood-fired oven and a sleek bar space, turning the joint into a hipster hangout where locals flock for bowling, brews, and the Flatbread Company's pizza concoctions.

During the *Ghost Hunters* investigation, then-co-owner Joseph Sacco claimed that a dark shadow would pass by him at a very high speed. Damon Sacco had similar scares. "My employees seem to think there are some weird things happening after hours," the then-co-owner spilled to the *Ghost Hunters* team. "I definitely heard some funky stuff at night." One guy quit because he felt something, or someone, behind him breathing on his neck.

According to the March 1, 2009, edition of the *Boston Globe*, Joseph Sacco heard "a real definitive footstep" at least four or five times coming from above the lanes when he worked the closing shift. "And then there's the dark shadow," he said, adding that a few times after the lights went off, a "mass would go flashing by me at very high speed."

Dee Morris, coauthor of *Somerville, Massachusetts: A Brief History*, was contacted by the paranormal investigative team. She didn't uncover any skeletons in Sacco's candlepin closet. However, she told the *Globe* that Davis Square "was very, very active in Revolutionary times," with a redcoat siege occurring on Willow Avenue. She also mentioned that Colonial-era Somervillians had a thing for lawn bowling and came up with the possibility that the sounds of pins falling at Sacco's had the potential of conjuring memories of the British ambush. Morris admitted that she may have thrown a gutter ball with the far-fetched theory.

Comedian and historian Jimmy Del Ponte came up with several paranormal scenarios. Perhaps it was the legendary Minnesota Fats, ticked off because a Somerville shark beat the pool player at his game during a heated round at Sacco's billiards area. There are also unsubstantiated reports of a murder at the after-hours nightclub formerly next door.

After the ghost-hunting equipment was packed away, the show's Atlantic Paranormal Society or TAPS team discovered that there were nonsupernatural explanations for most of the phenomena—for example, the so-called breathing noise heard by staffers turned out to be a leaky toilet. However, Sacco said that "they did find a few things that were bizarre," like "extraordinarily high levels of electromagnetic energy" in the space, which would explain the ghostly reports from former staff members.

Mike Brooks, a former manager at Flatbread Company, told me things have changed a lot since the ghost busters paid a visit: the pool table space was transformed into an open dining area, and there's been much turnover among the site's prerenovation employees. But one thing hasn't changed. Brooks has heard of a few "creepy encounters" from the staff, especially when the lights are turned off after closing.

In addition to Somerville, Malden is a city with an inexplicably large number of wayward spirits and residual hauntings.

Sure, it's not a typically haunted city and deviates a bit from the Lizzie Borden or Salem witch city norm. However, there's a historical legacy that's often overlooked by ghost hunters and para-celebs. It's also an easy Orange Line train ride from Boston and my home in Somerville's Assembly Row.

During the winter, I was covering an event in the old wing of the historic Malden Public Library. The well-preserved throwback to the Gilded Age was featured in the Mark Wahlberg movie *Ted 2* in 2015 and served as a creepy backdrop for the Travel Channel's *Dead Files* episode called "Dark Inheritance."

While taking photos for MATV's citizen journalism blog, I swore I spotted a chair move in the Converse Memorial Building as if an invisible force were taking a seat at the old-school library built in 1885.

"On its walls hang several of the paintings that were there when the building was dedicated in 1885," explained the library's website. "Most prominent is a full-length portrait of seventeen-year-old Frank Converse, in whose memory the library was constructed. On either side of him are his parents and the building's donors, Elisha and Mary Converse."

The Malden Public Library was recently featured in the movie *Ted 2* and served as a creepy backdrop for a Travel Channel's *Dead Files* episode called "Dark Inheritance."
PHOTO BY SAM BALTRUSIS

Was the spirit I encountered the ghost of the Converse teen? Digging through some historical research, it turns out that Frank Converse died tragically in what is believed to be the first bank robbery in America. The town's postmaster, Edward Green, was desperate for money, and on December 15, 1865, he trekked through the snowy streets of Malden to the city's bank located at 48 Pleasant Street. Green was there to make a usual deposit but noticed the teen was alone. The soon-to-be bank robber returned from the post office with his recently purchased Smith and Wesson pistol.

America's first bank robber shot Converse in the left temple. The boy fell to the ground, and Green, who stole five thousand dollars from the Malden Bank, shot Converse again.

The murder made national headlines. Green confessed to the grisly crime two months after the boy's body was discovered. Green was sentenced to death and hanged in April 1866. Converse's wealthy father, Elisha, became the first mayor of Malden in 1882 and erected the library three years later in honor of his slain son.

For the record, the murder occurred a stone's throw away from the library, which is located at 36 Salem Street. Others who visit the historic landmark claim to have encountered unseen forces that move furniture and even reach out to creeped-out patrons. "The library has a basement that contains books in different languages. I once went [there] and was looking for a certain book. All I could feel is a hand on the back of my neck," reported an anonymous source on the Ghosts of America website. "It bothered me so much. As soon as I moved a little, it stopped. Then after at least ten seconds, the hand went back on my neck, and it was the most terrifying thing I've ever experienced."

Sharon Santillo, a resident of the former Belmont School on Cross Street, says her fellow tenants encountered a ghost girl when they moved in fifteen years ago. "My condo building was converted from a school that had been built in the late 1800s and added onto in the 1930s," Santillo recalled. "All the tenants moved in around the same time, and two people on the ground floor saw a ghost of a young girl. She had long, dark hair and did not seem upset, nor were they frightened by her."

Santillo said the girl was spotted near the school's former theater. "Someone who had been a teacher in the building told us the area where she was seen had been the stage end of the cafeteria back when the building was a school," she said. "We made up a story about her that she had happily acted in school plays and came back to be in that place of good memories. But the conversion of the building took away that stage, and the girl has not been back since those early months, that I have heard about anyway."

Michael Baker, a well-respected paranormal investigator with Para-Boston and featured expert in my first book *Ghosts of Boston*, said Malden has several ghost stories including the "Lady in Grey" specter at Holy Cross Cemetery. "There is a ghostly hitchhiker that has been picked up several times only to disappear once she is inside the car," Baker said. "I know that is a popular theme for cemetery haunts, but this one comes from the 1960s."

There's also the legend of the mad scientist buried in Bell Rock Cemetery, which has a gravestone dating back to 1670, known as the Walking Corpse of Malden. The scientist experimented with chemicals to keep his postmortem flesh from rotting. "A group of people opened up the mad scientist's tomb after several years and were shocked and amazed to find that his flesh had not decayed as expected," according to the legend. "A medical student impetuously decided to sneak into the tomb that night and try to steal the corpse's head, but was tormented by apparitions and frantically ran out of the cemetery. He tossed the severed head into the tomb, and it is believed that a headless ghost walked the cemetery at night searching for its missing head."

Baker says he heard several creepy stories about the now-closed Malden Hospital being haunted. "A nurse friend of mine who passed away a few years ago used to tell me about crying that she would hear coming from a room that was vacant on the third floor," he recalled. "She told me that several other nurses noticed the nurse call light coming on from that room during the night shifts when the room was empty. She claims that she wasn't the only one to hear the crying and described it as a cry of pain . . . sort of a moaning." Baker continued: "She also said that the freight elevator would sometimes take you to the third floor no matter which floor number you hit."

The paranormal expert also overheard a ghost story at a store in the space formerly occupied by the Granada Theatre, located near the corner of Pleasant and Main Streets in Malden Square. "I overheard a couple of the employees talking about a sighting of a man with a cape and a strange hat," Baker recalls. "They were arguing about where they thought he was from. I then found out that what they were talking about was a ghostly apparition that one of the employees saw when they came in to open in the morning. The employee had to go home because she was so shaken up."

The former pharmacy was in the exact 21 Pleasant Street spot that housed the former Granada. For the record, the allegedly haunted theater closed in the mid-1980s and was later demolished after two girls snuck into the building in 1987 and set a fire that destroyed the historic structure.

Yes, the show must go on . . . even in the afterlife.

Conclusion

*One of the most frustrating and outlandish myths I've
encountered is the idea that people with genetic lineage related
to victims of the witch trials are somehow more magical.*
—Thomas O'Brien Vallor, Salem Tour Guide

While I was publicly writing about the ghosts associated with the Salem Witch Trials of 1692, my mother in Florida was secretly navigating the complexities of the genealogy of my family's maternal side using Ancestry.com. It was the day after I launched my second book on the Witch City called *Wicked Salem* when my mother dropped the bombshell.

"It looks like our ancestors had something to do with burning those witches," she told me with her thick Southern accent. I kindly corrected her. "Mom, they were hanged, not burned. But what did you find?"

My heart dropped when she started to rattle off names over the phone that I knew all too well. I'm a descendant of the Newport, Rhode Island, branch of the Gould family who migrated to the New World in the 1600s. At first, I thought we were in the clear. However, there was one Gould who played a pivotal role in the horrors that unfolded in Salem Village in 1692. My Puritan yeoman grandfather ten times removed had a sister, Priscilla Gould, who married John Putnam in 1611. If you know anything about the witch trials hysteria, you know the name Putnam. My Salem secret is that I'm related to both the Putnam and Gould families who owned land in two cities, Danvers and Topsfield, located in what was then called Salem Village in Massachusetts.

What really caused the deadliest witch hunt in American history? People who go on my walking tours or hear me lecture know my opinion. Yep, my Putnam cousins were responsible. They did it. And their land is stained with the blood of twenty innocent people. Salty tears started to flow down my cheeks. My paranormal journey over the past ten years—the scratches, the strange visitations, and ultimately the entity attachment in Topsfield featured on the Travel Channel's *A Haunting*—all made sense.

My family hunted witches.

Even if I was related to the afflicted girls of Salem Village, it doesn't necessarily mean it gave me any special insight into the hysteria. Or did it?

"One of the most frustrating and outlandish myths I've encountered is the idea that people with genetic lineage related to victims of the witch trials are somehow more magical," tour guide Thomas O'Brien Vallor told me while writing *Wicked Salem*. "The victims of the witch trials were definitely not witches. No educated person in Salem or elsewhere believes that they were, but there is a small amount of annoying people who think they were."

While I don't believe my familial lineage made me more magical, I do believe it explained my weird obsession with the deadliest witch hunt in American history. Do I have a history of trying to make amends for the sins of my forefathers? Yes, and I didn't even know I was related.

In hindsight, my relationship with the ghosts of Salem's witch trials past has intensified over the past few years. I started to notice a recurring theme with the spirits that I've encountered along the way. A few of the innocent victims from the witchcraft hysteria were reaching out to me.

And they've been dead for more than three centuries.

In 2012, I had a ghostly encounter with the first person to be hanged during the 1692 witch trials and the only one to be executed alone: Bridget Bishop. Soon after I penned my first paranormal-themed history book, I signed on to give walking tours of my own in a city that both excited and terrified me. I let Salem's spirits guide me. I had several odd experiences outside of Lyceum Hall, which was said to be Bishop's tavern. However, it was her

Photo by Frank C. Grace

Opened in 1816 and used as headquarters for the city's government until 1837, Old Town Hall is known for its ghostly inhabitants wearing period garb.

orchard. An apple mysteriously rolled out of nowhere in the alley behind what is now Turner's Seafood. I looked up. No one was there.

Was Bishop correcting my historically inaccurate retelling of her story? At the time, I believed it was her. I accepted it as a peace offering from the innocent woman often misportrayed in pop culture as an overtly sexual tavern owner.

For several years, the Witch City's ghosts took a break. No contact. But the hiatus didn't last for long.

In 2016, I signed on to give the "Myths & Misconceptions" tour, which focused more on history and less on Salem's ghosts.

On one of the history tours, a woman from California flipped out when I spoke in front of Salem's Town Hall. Home to the reenactment of Bridget Bishop's trial called "Cry Innocent," the historic structure is famous for the dance sequence in the movie *Hocus Pocus*. It's also where I launched my third book, *Ghosts of Salem: Haunts of the Witch City*. The out-of-town visitor on my tour swore she saw two ghostly faces pressed against the window on the second floor of Town Hall as if they were intently listening to what I said. I nodded when she told me. "Yep, I know the ghosts of Salem are listening," I said followed by a nervous laugh. She had no clue what I'd seen.

Nestled next to the highly trafficked Charter Street Cemetery in Salem, the Samuel Pickman House is now owned by the Peabody Essex Museum. Tour groups pass this historic building, and passersby peek through its windows. Several people believe they've seen a full-bodied apparition of a girl peering from the upper-floor window. Others claim the small Colonial-era structure is home to a demonic entity that manifests in photos taken through the seventeenth-century building's old-school windows.

One ghastly story tells of a husband and wife who lived in the Samuel Pickman House with their seven-year-old daughter. Similar to the demonic infestation in Stephen King's *The Shining*, an evil entity is rumored to have caused the husband to go insane.

According to legend, the man chained his daughter in the attic, torturing and starving the child. He then tied his wife to a tree outside and killed her by pouring hot wax over her body, leaving her to die a slow, painful death. The possessed man then fled, leaving the dead child in the attic and his murdered-by-wax wife tied to the tree.

People on my walking tours who have taken photos of the house claim it is still inhabited by a demonic force. There are many reports of the ghost of the young girl looking out the attic window at the crowds below.

PHOTO BY FRANK C. GRACE

The Samuel Pickman House, located on the corner of Charter and Liberty Streets, is said to be home to an evil entity connected to a horrific murder committed centuries ago.

After doing exhaustive historical research, I found no real proof to suggest that the story of the murder or the supposed demonic infestation at the house is true. However, the building is a surefire hot spot of photographic anomalies, ranging from orbs to a mist that envelops the structure.

Next to the Samuel Pickman House is the Witch Trials Memorial and the old cemetery. My most profound encounter in Salem several years ago was at the Old Burying Point on Charter Street. I spotted a full-bodied apparition of a lady in white coming from what I learned later was the gravestone of Giles Corey's second wife, Mary. It's my theory that Mary Corey's residual energy is looking for her husband. She's heading oddly toward the very spot located at the present-day Howard Street Cemetery, where the stubborn but determined old man was crushed to death. Yes, love does exist in the afterlife.

In 2018, when I was doing some last-minute research for *Wicked Salem*, I felt compelled to visit the recently discovered hanging site of the nineteen innocent men and woman executed during the witch hysteria. It was two days after the anniversary of Rebecca Nurse's hanging, which was July 21, 1692. While I was taking photos of the memorial at Proctor's Ledge, a woman holding a bag came up to me and asked: "So, what is this all about? What happened here?"

Her complexion was ruddy, almost as if she was weathered by the sun and the harsh elements of New England. If I had to guess, she was either homeless or a transient carrying all her belongings in the bag hanging over her shoulder. The woman was young, in her late thirties, but appeared much older.

She reminded me of a modern-day version of Sarah Good. The town beggar woman was thirty-eight when she was hanged at Proctor's Ledge. She was also the first to be interrogated for witchcraft during the trials and, on the day of my visit in July 2018, it was Good's birthday.

I told the mystery woman that it was Proctor's Ledge, the location where nineteen innocent men and women were hanged for witchcraft more than 300 years ago. She looked at me, sort of shocked. "I never heard of such a thing," she responded, adding that she's from up North and doesn't know much about the area.

I was taken aback, surprised that she had never heard of the Salem Witch Trials. Then I asked for her name. "Sarah," she said as I was pointing to the rocky crevices, showing her where the victims

A memorial at Proctor's Ledge honors the nineteen innocent victims of the witch trials in Salem, including Bridget Bishop and Sarah Good.

Photo by Sam Baltrusis

were likely dumped into a shallow grave. Beneath my feet was a message carved in stone: "We remember."

I looked behind me to respond to the woman, and she was gone. Vanished. Into thin air.

What's going on and why am I being visited by the ghosts of Salem's past? I reached out to Jack Kenna, a paranormal investigator and author featured on TV shows like *Paranormal Survivor* and *Haunted Case Files*. He believes there's an "inhuman" entity lurking in the shadows of the Witch City that may be responsible for the ghostly visitations.

"There's something much older and much more intense that resides in the Salem area," Kenna told me. "It likes to pretend it is something other than it is, and while I would not call it demonic, I would say it has a dislike of humans and is something that I would call elemental in its nature. In other words, it is inhuman."

Kenna believes the Witch City has an "aura of disaster" that has left a psychic imprint. "Like most of New England, there is a lot of history in Salem," he said. "Some of its history is good and some very tragic."

The paranormal investigator said tragedies preceding the witch trials of 1692 stained the land with blood. "In 1615, the Naumkeag tribe engaged in war with the Tarrantine people, which cost the lives of many on both sides," he explained. "Then in 1617, a plague broke out in the region that took a heavy toll on the Naumkeag people."

Kenna said the smallpox epidemic in the 1630s devastated Salem's native population, which tainted the soil in the years leading up to the witch trials. "Then in 1830, one of the most infamous murders in early American history took place in Salem, the murder of Captain Joseph White by Richard Crowninshield," he said. "If there ever was a town that had cause to be haunted, it would be Salem."

The author of *S.P.I.R.I.T.S. of New England: Hauntings, Ghosts & Demons* said his empathic abilities are heightened in the Witch City. "Having spent some time in Salem in recent years and being able to participate in investigations at locations in town, I have picked up on something more than just human spirit and the residual energies of past events in these locations," he said.

What exactly is an "elemental" entity, which Kenna believes is hiding in Salem's shadows? "They are an ancient inhuman spirit that is directly connected to the elements of our world . . . earth, wind, fire, and water," Kenna explained, adding that Native Americans worshipped these ancient elementals, and they are still revered by native tribes. "They are not demons or angels. Elementals don't try to physically harm humans, but they typically don't like modern humans because of the way we treat the world."

Yes, it would make sense that an elemental entity was lurking in the shadows of Salem.

In April 2019, I returned to Witch City to work for Salem Historical Tours. I met with the tour owner, Giovanni Alabiso, and he said that a shadow figure was spotted in the office. In fact, he said a voice asked, "When is he coming back?" and he automatically assumed that it somehow was related to me because of my reputation as the Witch City's ghost guy.

As the weeks progressed, Salem started to get progressively dark for me. A paperweight hurled off the shelf toward me one afternoon. My coworkers were shocked. Multiple tour guides reported seeing a black mist followed by a shadow figure wearing a hat in the office. "I heard something tonight, and it sounded like it was behind me, but that would be the wall," Alabiso told me. "It sounded like a scraping noise. It wasn't me. I like the idea that the place has history and spirits, but it seems like this is becoming problematic."

The last straw for me was when I heard footsteps walk up the stairs leading to the office on Central Street. When I looked down near the front-entrance door, I saw that same shadow figure with the hat leering beneath the stairs. The activity was intensifying, and I couldn't make it stop.

At this point, I felt like I was being stalked. The following week, I decided to take a break. The short-term goal was to stop giving ghost tours until I figured out why I was being pushed out of Salem by this inhuman entity. Did it have anything to do with the fact that I was related to the Putnams?

I reached out to my friend and noted demonologist James Annitto. "It's my understanding through documentation, theories, and my own experiences that the 'hat man' tends to linger at areas of death or highly active locations," Annitto told me. "They're usually not malevolent and only become hostile if they're bothered. They tend to watch."

I came up with a game plan after chatting with Annitto. I decided to apologize for the sins of my ancestors. I found what some historians labeled a "fauxpology" from my cousin, Ann Putnam Jr., who was the primary "afflicted girl" responsible for accusing Rebecca Nurse, her sisters, and several others of witchcraft when she was twelve years old.

Putnam begged the Reverend Green to allow her back in the church seven years after losing both of her parents in 1699. The young minister crafted and then read what seemed like a heartfelt confession supposedly coming from the then twenty-nine-year-old Putnam, claiming that she was an unwitting pawn of Satan and wrongfully accused the innocent men and women of witchcraft in 1692. "I, then being in my childhood, should, by such a providence of God, be made an instrument for the accusing of several persons of a grievous crime, whereby their lives were taken away from them," Green read from the pulpit, "whom now I have just grounds and good reason to believe they were innocent persons."

After it was publicly read in 1706, Putnam agreed to these crimes against humanity and then said that she "desired to lie in the dust and be humbled for it." My cousin was allowed back in the church but continued to be ostracized by the Salem Village community. She died a single woman eight years later.

When I suggested to Annitto that my plan was to read Putnam's confession at a location significant to the witch trials hysteria, the Old Catholic Church deacon told me that he thought it was a good idea. "Maybe you can read something similar but in your own words," Annitto said. "Present an apology, but speak from your heart."

I then contacted my Wiccan high-priestess friend, Dana Masson, a direct descendant of witch trials victim Elizabeth Howe. She agreed to help me facilitate my updated apology for my Putnam relatives, but where would we go? The initial plan was to perform the ritual at Proctor's Ledge, the spot where historians believe that nineteen innocent men and women were hanged for witchcraft in 1692.

However, something didn't feel quite right about the craggy-rock location behind the Walgreens on Boston Street. I asked her to meet me at the train station in Salem one morning in September 2019 and suggested that we let the spirits guide us to the appropriate place. Masson agreed.

Armed with my revised version of Putnam's apology and an arsenal of supplies that included white sage, a Palo Santo stick, a lemongrass braid, coffin nails, and an abalone shell, I arrived at Salem Depot eager to make amends. As soon as I stepped off the train, I decided to drop my backpack and pray for guidance.

When I opened my eyes, a black bird emerged from the clouds. It turns out that I was surrounded by a murder of crows.

PHOTO BY FRANK C. GRACE

The city dedicated a new memorial at Proctor's Ledge, the spot where historians believe that nineteen innocent men and women were hanged for witchcraft in 1692.

They quickly took flight and headed in a direction that appeared to be north. My first instinct was that we were being led to the Rebecca Nurse Homestead in neighboring Danvers, which was known as Salem Village in 1692.

I walked over to Masson, a good friend who had gone on my walking tours in Salem and investigated the Parson Barnard House with me in North Andover. She sheepishly waved from the depot's parking lot. I told her about my encounter with the crows, and, after changing the car's destination on her dashboard, she started driving toward 149 Pine Street near the Northshore Mall.

In hindsight, we didn't really know where we were going, but it felt like we were being led somewhere.

We pulled into the Rebecca Nurse Homestead even though it appeared to be closed. The caretaker greeted us outside of the Colonial-era saltbox home, and our hunch was correct. We were hoping to check out the cemetery located on the property. No luck. The area was off-limits because they were repairing the historic gravestones.

Based on my August 2018 visit to the family plot located behind the Nurse property, I strongly believe that the land is haunted, specifically near the memorial, which also includes the remains of several Putnam family members. Walking into the Nurse family burial ground, you could feel an energy shift. I also sensed a male presence there and actually saw an outline of a man when I shot photos of the gravestone of witch trials victim George Jacobs Sr.

It felt like someone was peering at me from the woods behind the burial ground.

As we pulled out of the Rebecca Nurse Homestead, the caretaker suggested several alternatives in Danvers, including the Putnam Cemetery on Maple Street. Masson and I decided to drive around the area and let our spirit guides lead the way.

We passed the Witchcraft Victims' Memorial on Hobart Street and noticed a blue plaque for the Samuel Parris Archaeological Site on Centre Street. We cautiously pulled up to the marker that read "Pass at your own risk."

There was a dirt road next to an old house. A large bird, possibly a hawk, flew above us. It was a sign . . . literally.

We slowly approached ground zero of what became the initial affliction that swept throughout Salem Village in February 1692 affecting nine-year-old Betty Parris, who barked like a dog and cried out in pain, followed by her eleven-year-old cousin, Abigail Williams, who also lived in the house and started exhibiting similar symptoms.

As I descended the rock-encrusted stairs into the foundation of what was the Reverend Samuel Parris's parsonage, Masson read out loud the text on the memorial marker. It reminded me that the Reverend George Burroughs, who was hanged for witchcraft on August 19, 1692, actually lived in the church-owned house when he was minister of Salem Village from 1680 to 1683.

Masson joined me in the pit and created what she called a "sacred space," an area used for Wiccan ritual. As she cast the circle with sea salt, I felt the energy shift in the subterranean area hidden behind a copse of trees. I reached for my bag of supplies, which included some smudging basics like sage and feathers as well as the recrafted apology of my cousin taking responsibility for her role in the Salem Witch Trials.

Salem, Massachusetts, is famous for its 1692 witch trials, during which several locals were executed for allegedly practicing witchcraft.

As I proceeded to read the words out loud, I felt like we weren't alone. Masson and I both believed that there were spirits joining us in the magic circle. In hindsight, my Wiccan friend said that she was connecting with Tituba, the Parris family's slave originally from Barbados.

"I had Tituba on my mind on the way there, but when I set foot on that land, I could really feel her," Masson told me. "She never got over the guilt of feeling that she started the whole thing."

As I continued to speak, I felt a male spirit walk up next to me. He was wearing a hat. As he inched closer, I had the ultimate realization standing in the hearth of the Parris foundation. It was the Reverend George Burroughs, and he was listening to me.

My head started to spin. Was Burroughs the "hat man" that I'd encountered in Salem? When I asked for a sign, I got a confirmation of sorts. I heard the bell from the nearby First Church of

Danvers ring. I felt like the reverend was letting me know that all was forgiven.

While Masson was closing the magic circle, I burned a braid of lemongrass as an offering and then inserted a coffin nail in the ground to signify closure. We both felt an immediate shift in the energy from an inexplicable heaviness to a feeling of peace.

"We followed the breadcrumbs and it was perfect," Masson said smiling. "I'm so proud of us finding where we needed to go." We heard what sounded like a bird whistling from the trees behind us. For the first time since finding out that I was related to the Putnams, I took a deep breath and exhaled. Apology accepted.

Acknowledgments

When I write my books, I sometimes must go to a dark place. I dive into the abyss not knowing if I will resurface.

I took a leap of faith with *Mass Murders* and reemerged with a completely different perspective of what I thought was the truth. I initially planned to write a book that revisited Massachusetts-based murder cases using a paranormal lens. However, that quickly changed. The core of this book is about untangling fact from fiction and then weaving together a cohesive narrative of the players involved in some of the more infamous and lesser-known cases.

The section called "The Legends" explored a handful of the tall tales that have been planted long ago in the hard soil of early Puritan thought. What's interesting is that some of the true crime stories featured in "The Notorious" and "The Forgotten" had similar not-so-accurate themes staining their "just the facts" façade.

Yes, even back then the truth was much stranger than fiction. Meanwhile, New England's rigid sense of morality skewed some of these stories involving murder and mayhem, and the backstory became twisted over time to reflect generational biases.

The nineteenth-century gossip mill that demonized accused child killer Bathsheba Sherman, for example, fed into the "Satanic Panic" of the 1970s. The result was a supposed witch who sacrificed youngsters to the Devil in a not-so-true depiction that terrorized modern filmgoers with *The Conjuring*.

If you look at the real woman behind the character, Sherman's backstory wasn't an open-and-shut case.

One of the highlights of writing *Mass Murders* was my interview with Andrea Perron. Her family's real-life story inspired the movie. Contrary to what I initially believed, Perron didn't hold a grudge against Bathsheba. Why? The *House of Darkness House of Light* author doesn't blame the not-so-sinister spirit for what her sisters and mother endured.

"We were told way in advance. We knew *The Conjuring* was a piece of fiction," Perron told me. "Our real story was so intense that they couldn't use it."

I mentioned to Perron that it upset me that the movie suggested that Mary Easty, a victim of the 1692 witch trials hysteria in Salem, secretly practiced witchcraft and then passed down her family's tricks of the trade. In fact, the movie's fictionalized version of the late, great Lorraine Warren claimed that Sherman's demon spirit was a descendant of Easty.

"Well, it upsets me to see my mother in the movie hovering over my baby sister, April, with a pair of scissors," Perron shot back. "My mother thought it was so ridiculous that it was laughable."

I'm grateful for all the people I interviewed for this book in addition to Perron, including Sue Vickery, Bill Pavao, Rachel Hoffman, Peter Muise, Thomas D'Agostino, Joni Mayhan, Cindy Vallar, Sandra Lee, James Annitto, Jack Kenna, Cheryl Cesarini, Christopher Balzano, Ian Judge, and Dana Masson. Special thanks to Gare Allen for penning the book's foreword.

Photographers Jason Baker and Frank C. Grace deserve a supernatural slap on the back for capturing the eerie aesthetic of the main haunts featured in this book. I would also like to thank Amy Lyons from Globe Pequot for her support during the process of putting *Mass Murders* together.

Thanks to my mother, Deborah Hughes Dutcher, for her investigative work uncovering our familial ties to the Putnams, and my family and friends for their continued support.

For the record, my skills as a journalist and editor were important for the gumshoe approach to the crime-related stories featured in *Mass Murders*. I double checked the ABCs—or "accuracy," "brevity," and "clarity"—that I needed to effectively reexamine the historic cases featured in *Mass Murders*. Some of the best advice came with a K.I.S.S. or "keep it simple, stupid" that was reinforced by historians like Bill Pavao, who reminded me that it's important not to overcomplicate cases like the Borden murders in Fall River, Massachusetts.

My goal was to give a voice to the victims and, in a few cases, the villains featured in this book. *Mass Murders* is for them. I hope I did them justice.

Sources

Updated excerpts from my first twelve books, including *Ghost Writers: The Hallowed Haunts of Unforgettable Literary Icons*, *Wicked Salem: Exploring Lingering Lore and Legends*, *13 Most Haunted in Massachusetts*, and *Haunted Boston Harbor* were featured in *Mass Murders: Bloodstained Crime Scenes Haunting the Bay State*.

The material in this book was drawn from published sources, including my articles in *DigBoston* and issues of the *Berkshire Eagle*, *Boston Globe*, *Boston Herald*, *Boston Phoenix*, the *Enterprise*, the *Gloucester Telegraph*, *Herald News*, the *New York Times*, North Andover's *Eagle-Tribune*, the *Observer*, *Salem News*, *Salem Evening News*, *SouthCoast Today*, *Zagat*, and television programs like the Travel Channel's *Ghost Adventures*, *Most Terrifying Places*, *Kindred Spirits*, *A Haunting*, and *Ghost Hunters* formerly on Syfy. Several books on New England's paranormal history were used and cited throughout the text. Other New England–based websites and periodicals, like Peter Muise's *New England Folklore*, WHDH.com, MassLive, and Ghosts of America, as well as the websites for the Malden Public Library and National Park Service, served as sources.

Several of the experts featured in *Mass Murders* like Andrea Perron, Christopher Balzano, Gare Allen, Jack Kenna, Joni Mayhan,

PHOTO BY JASON BAKER

Inmate files from the historic Ash Street Jail located in New Bedford, Massachusetts. Lizzie Borden stayed in the facility's matrons' quarters for twelve days awaiting her trial in 1893.

Peter Muise, Sandra Lee, and Thomas D'Agostino are also authors. I highly recommend their books as supplemental reading.

For most of *Mass Murders*, I conducted firsthand interviews, and some of the material was drawn from my own research. My former history-based tours, Wicked Salem (hosted at Wicked Good Books), Boston Haunts, and my Harvard Square Ghost Tour were also major sources and generated original content. It should be noted that ghost stories are subjective, and I have made a concerted effort to stick to the historical facts, even if it resulted in debunking an alleged encounter with the paranormal.

Baltrusis, Sam. *Ghosts of Boston: Haunts of the Hub*. Charleston, SC: History Press, 2012.

———. *Ghosts of Salem: Haunts of the Witch City*. Charleston, SC: History Press, 2014.

———. *Haunted Boston Harbor*. Charleston, SC: History Press, 2016.

———. *13 Most Haunted Crime Scenes Beyond Boston*. Boston, MA: Sam Baltrusis, 2016.

———.*Ghost Writers: The Hallowed Haunts of Unforgettable Literary Icons*. Guilford, CT: Globe Pequot, 2019.

———. *Wicked Salem: Exploring Lingering Lore and Legends*. Guilford, CT: Globe Pequot, 2019.

Balzano, Christopher. *Dark Woods: Cults, Crime, and the Paranormal in the Freetown State Forest, Massachusetts*. Atglen, PA: Schiffer Publishing, 2007.

Boyer, Paul, and Stephen Nissenbaum. *Salem Possessed: The Social Origins of Witchcraft*. Cambridge, MA: Harvard University Press, 1974.

Cahill, Robert Ellis. *New England's Ghostly Haunts*. Peabody, MA: Chandler-Smith Publishing, 1983.

———. *Haunted Happenings*. Salem, MA: Old Saltbox Publishing House, 1992.

———. *New England's Witches and Wizards*. Peabody, MA: Chandler-Smith Publishing, 1983.

Carr, Howie. *The Brothers Bulger*. New York: Time Warner, 2006.

D'Agostino, Thomas. *A Guide to Haunted New England*. Charleston, SC: History Press, 2009.

D'Entremont, Jeremy. *The Lighthouse Handbook New England*. Kennebunkport, ME: Cider Mill Press, 2016.

Dudley, Dorothy. *Theatrum Majorum: The Cambridge of 1776*. Whitefish, MT: Kessinger Publishing, 2007.

Ford, Beverly, and Stephanie Schorow. *The Boston Mob Guide*. Charleston, SC: History Press, 2011.

Forest, Christopher. *North Shore Spirits of Massachusetts*. Atglen, PA: Schiffer Publishing, 2003.

Guiley, Rosemary Ellen. *Haunted Salem*. Mechanicsburg, PA: Stackpole Books, 2011.

Hall, Thomas. *Shipwrecks of Massachusetts Bay*. Charleston, SC: History Press, 2012.

Hauk, Dennis William. *Haunted Places: The National Directory*. New York: Penguin Group, 1996.

Hill, Frances. *Hunting for Witches*. Carlisle, MA: Commonwealth Editions, 2002.

Jasper, Mark. *Haunted Inns of New England*. Yarmouthport, MA: On Cape Publications, 2000.

Kampas, Barbara Pero. *The Great Fire of 1914*. Charleston, SC: History Press, 2008.

Macken, Lynda Lee. *Haunted Salem & Beyond*. Forked River, NJ: Black Cat Press, 2001.

Mayhan, Joni. *Dark and Scary Things*. Gardner, MA: Joni Mayhan, 2015.

Muise, Peter. *Legends and Lore of the North Shore*. Charleston, SC: History Press, 2014.

Nadler, Holly Mascott. *Ghosts of Boston Town: Three Centuries of True Hauntings*. Camden, ME: Down East Books, 2002.

Perron, Andrea. *House of Darkness, House of Light*. Bloomington, IN: AuthorHouse, 2011.

Powers, Edwin. *Crime and Punishment in Early Massachusetts*. Boston, MA: Beacon Press, 1966.

Rapaport, Diane. *The Naked Quaker: True Crimes and Controversies*. Beverly, MA: Commonwealth Editions, 2007.

Revai, Cheri. *Haunted Massachusetts: Ghosts and Strange Phenomena of the Bay State*. Mechanicsburg, PA: Stackpole Books, 2005.

Rule, Leslie. *When the Ghost Screams: True Stories of Victims Who Haunt*. Kansas City, MO: Andrews McMeel Publishing, 2006.

Sweester, M. F. *King's Handbook of Boston Harbor*. Boston, MA: Houghton, Mifflin & Co., 1888.

Tucker, Elizabeth. *Haunted Halls: Ghostlore of American College Campuses*. Jackson: University Press of Mississippi, 2007.

Weeks, Kevin, and Phyllis Kara. *Brutal: My Life Inside Whitey Bulger's Irish Mob*. New York: HarperCollins, 2006.

Wilhelm, Robert. *Murder & Mayhem in Essex County*. Charleston, SC: History Press, 2011.

Zwicker, Roxie J. *Haunted Pubs of New England: Raising Spirits of the Past*. Charleston, SC: History Press, 2007.

Index

About the Author

Sam Baltrusis, author of *Ghost Writers: The Hallowed Haunts of Unforgettable Literary Icons*, has penned twelve historical-based ghost books including *Mass Murders: Bloodstained Crime Scenes Haunting the Bay State.* He has been featured on several national TV shows including the Travel Channel's *Most Terrifying Places*, *Haunted Towns*, and *Haunted USA* on Salem and served as Boston's paranormal expert on the Biography Channel's *Haunted Encounters.* In

PHOTO COURTESY OF FRANK C. GRACE

Doppelgänger? Author Sam Baltrusis specializes in historical haunts and has been featured on several national television shows sharing his experiences with the paranormal.

2019, he was featured on the 100th episode of *A Haunting* that aired on the Travel Channel. Baltrusis is a sought-after lecturer who speaks at dozens of paranormal-related events scattered throughout New England, including an author discussion at the Massachusetts State House and paranormal conventions that he produced including the Berkshire's MASS ParaCon in 2019 and the Plymouth ParaCon in 2020. In the past, he has worked for VH1, MTV.com, *Newsweek*, and ABC Radio, and as a regional stringer for the *New York Times*. Visit SamBaltrusis.com for more information.